The Family Video Guide

Terry and Catherine Catchpole

Williamson Publishing
Charlotte, Vermont

**Library of Congress
Cataloging-in-Publication Data**

Catchpole, Terry, 1941-
    The Family Video Guide: Over 300 Movies
    to Share with Your Children/Terry Catchpole and
    Catherine Catchpole.
        p.   cm.
    Includes bibliographical references (p.169) and index.
    ISBN 0-913589-64-0
    1. Motion pictures – Catalogs.   2. Video recordings –
Catalogs.   3. Motion pictures and children.   4. Motion pictures –
Moral and ethical aspects.   I. Catchpole, Catherine, 1944-   . II
Title.
PN1998.C34   1992
016.79143'75 – dc20   91-46899
                                                            CIP

Cover design: Trezzo-Braren Studio
Typesetting: Superior Type
Printing: Capital City Press

Williamson Publishing Co.
Box 185
Charlotte, Vermont 05445
(800) 234-8791

Manufactured in the United States of America

10 9 8 7 6 5 4 3 2 1

Acknowledgements

For helping to bring this book into being, we thank Al Zuckerman of The Writer's House and Susan Williamson of Williamson Publishing, Inc., and our friend Don Lessem, for being such an excellent matchmaker.

For nurturing our commentary on movies over the past few years, we thank the following editors for their encouragement and support: Susan Chomsky, David Hajdu, Peter Kobel, and Jim Meigs at *Entertainment Weekly;* Bruce Apar, Lou Mulkern, and Andy Wickstrom at *Video Business;* and Terry Byrne and Bill Weber at the *Boston Herald,* where much of this material originally appeared.

Contents

Introduction

We bought our first VCR in 1984, when our children were ages ten and five, and video stores were beginning to sprout on city street corners and suburban malls. The two movies we watched on our first night in The Video Age were *True Grit* and *The Man Who Would Be King,* and the experience set in motion an approach to video viewing that we have adhered to since.

Our children loved those two movies, and over the following seven years they have come to love many other movies made before they – and sometimes their parents – were born. Instead of watching only children's movies or the latest popular video releases, we watched the classics of the recent and not-so-recent past and discovered an important lesson that applies to movies and any other creative medium: quality is timeless. Quality movies of any period will appeal to kids today just as the plays of Shakespeare and the art of van Gogh have had an enduring appeal for young audiences.

Watching great movies provided us with a terrific entertainment experience. The ritual of the Friday night pizza and classic film left us with a lifetime's worth of shared memories – our Americanized family-room version of *Cinema Paradiso.*

But the experience also gave our children an appreciation for quality filmmaking and an interest in the actors, directors, and writers involved in the movies we watched together. Today their all-time favorite movie list includes titles such as *Topper, Duck Soup, On the Waterfront, Harvey,* and *The Man Who Shot Liberty Valance.* (See page 32 for a complete listing of their favorites.)

There was yet another value to this approach to video viewing, one that had an even greater bearing on our immediate family: watching these movies provided us with an excellent common ground on which to base family conversations. With a particular movie as a reference point, these conversations could range over history, culture, social trends, politics, and human behavior.

Watching *All the President's Men,* for example, prompted a discussion of Watergate, Nixon, and the role of the press in our society. *The Glenn Miller Story* provided the background for a conversation on rock and roll's antecedents in the swing bands and jazz groups of the 1930s. *The Year of Living Dangerously* opened the door to talk of political, social, and economic conditions in the Third World and how Western nations deal with them. *Yankee Doodle Dandy* taught us about vaudeville, *Sunset Boulevard* about moviemaking, and *My Favorite Year* about the early days of television.

Indeed, dinnertime often found us discussing any number of movies from any number of angles, as well as playing guessing games involving movie characters, scenes, and quotes. And we kept handily posted a continually changing list of favorite movie performers and our all-time top ten films.

Knowing that we were movie fans and frequent video viewers, other parents were soon asking us for suggestions on what they might watch with their children. Frequently this was expressed as something like this: "We've had it up to here with *The Gumdrop Girls Get a Pony* or *Kickboxing Creeps from Outer Space.* Isn't there *anything* else?"

We would tell them of our experience and suggest that they might try a movie like, say, *Casablanca* as a starter. "But," they would plead, "that's a black-and-white adult romance from the 1940s. And the stars are all dead!"

All true, we would answer, but to kids it's an exciting wartime adventure, with Resistance fighters, spies, missing letters of transit, secret meetings, Nazi soldiers, midnight planes, and a funny fat guy with a parrot.

They tried it, the kids loved it, and another family was hooked on using movie video pro-actively, as a shared adventure.

What we and the other families discovered is a contemporary truism that we now happily share with you in this book: VCRs and movies on video provide parents and children with access to a new kind of family experience — watching the great movies of the past and enjoying them for both their entertainment and personal enrichment.

Young people growing up today are charter members of the video generation, the first generation to come of age with instant access to virtually all of the greatest movies ever made. Put another way, the treasury of seventy-plus years of Hollywood moviemaking is no farther away than a local video store or a mail-order 800 number. And the parents of this generation also have an unprecedented opportunity — that of sharing with their children the experience of randomly and willfully sampling from this spectacular cornucopia.

By taking creative advantage of thousands of movies available on video, families can explore important cultural and historical subjects, open up wide-ranging channels of communication, and watch terrific movies in the process. All that's required is commitment – and some help negotiating racks full of unfamiliar or dimly remembered titles. That's where we come in.

Now a few words about this book:

* This is a collection of 300-plus movies selected primarily for their insights into the world in which we live and for their bearing on the general topical themes discussed in chapter 5. By and large, they are outstanding movies and include many of the best ever made. However, it is also important to note that many films of exceptional quality are not included and this list is not intended to be taken as a "best ever" compendium.

* Our descriptions of movies in this book are meant to help potential viewers identify titles they want to have a look at and then to put those movies into some thematic context. Our descriptions do not submit the films to thorough review, analysis, or probing critique. Other books do this well.

* We also provide an extensive list of "For Starters" films in chapter 4. These movies are especially recommended for families with younger children.

* This book is meant to encourage readers/viewers to explore and sample seventy years of great moviemaking. You may find some of the supposedly "great movies" boring and some of the supposed disasters entertaining. Home video movies are the most pluralistic, democratic form of popular entertainment since network television: you control what you watch, and when and how you watch it. This book is intended to help you take full advantage of this phenomenon.

* The operative thought behind this book is that movies are supposed to be, above all else, an entertainment medium, meant to amuse, excite, terrify, and/or enlighten millions of people. Yes, it's interesting to probe the inner meanings of individual movies, but it's more important that people kick back and have a good time watching them. Here the idea is that parents and children will watch them together. If your child should happen to become a serious film buff in the process, great.

* This book has movies for all ages, but not all the movies discussed here are for all ages. Some, in fact, are recommended only for older

teenagers. Parents are encouraged to read the rating information and recommendations in the capsule reviews in chapter 6 carefully, and make viewing decisions based on their individual family situations. What's most important is that parents watch the movies with their children, so if sensitive material is presented, they are there to defuse or explain it.

* Most of the movies here are rated G, PG, and PG-13. Ten of the 300-plus movies are rated R. The truth is that we would rather have our children watch an occasional R-rated movie whose infrequent profanity, violence, or sexual content is placed in a believable context, than have them subjected to some hot-ticket blockbuster slasher with a body count in the hundreds and violence that demeans humankind. The major failing of many contemporary movies, we feel, is not their language or gaping flesh wounds, it's that they treat their audience (especially teenagers) like mindless, emotionless garbage.

Our final message to parents is simply this: Enjoy these movies. Experiment. Investigate actors with whom you are not familiar or themes that you've never had time to consider. In a short time, your family will come to think of many of these movies as old friends. Like old friends, you will look forward to "meeting" them again and again, each time finding some new facet or nuance to savor. Such are the joys of video viewing.

There is also no doubt that you have – or will soon find – some family favorites that you would like to see listed here because you think other families will enjoy them as well. Great! One reason they might not be here is that we haven't gotten around to seeing them yet. So drop us a note, c/o Williamson Publishing, Box 185, Charlotte, VT 05445, describing your favorites, and we'll be happy to consider them for inclusion in the next edition of this book.

Psssst! Secret Message to Grandparents

Hey – you grew up watching a lot of these movies as children yourselves! You know all about James Cagney, Katharine Hepburn, and Cary Grant. You know the actors, the stories, and the settings, and you know all about the magical charm they hold for young people. You know it because you once felt it!

So now, what about your grandchildren? What better bonding experience than to spend a couple of hours together, just you and them, watching a great comedy or adventure movie that you first discovered in your childhood. You get to share your memories and insights with your grandchildren. They get introduced to a whole new world of magical entertainment, with you as their friendly guide. And you both get an experience to treasure.

This book gives grandparents plenty of tips on how and where to get started with this experience, and before long, you'll have plenty of ideas of your own. You might begin by making up a priority or "A-list" of movies you'd like to watch with your grandchildren. Then take this list to some local video stores and browse around to see who has the best collection of older titles, or which store managers seem most willing to order them.

If you socialize regularly with other grandparents, formally or informally, you might suggest that the group jointly purchase selected popular titles and then pass them around for viewing with grandchildren (the price for most titles in this book is less than $20). Or, you could represent your group to a local video store owner and suggest that your group's regular patronage would make it worthwhile for them to purchase selected "classic" titles. You might even offer to work with them on special promotions of "family classic" titles.

Before you know it, "Movie Night" with the grandchildren will become a regular staple in your lives. Welcome to the Video Age!

You Expect Me To Watch That?

Two things need to happen for children to enjoy quality classic and contemporary movies and for parents to enjoy the movies with them:

1. Parents need the confidence to guide the children through the viewing experience.

2. Children need exposure to quality movies in the most positive atmosphere possible.

This is easier said than done. If you and/or your children have been watching a steady diet of blockbuster A-list hits, with the occasional Schwarzenegger "classic" thrown in, then it will be all but impossible to switch suddenly to a black-and-white movie comedy from the 1930s starring good old what's-his-name.

First of all, you might be nervous about the switch, which addresses step number one: Parents must be confident in the quality of a movie and the viewing experience before they invite their children to watch it with them. If the parents are nervous, uncertain, and tentative, the children are sure to pick up on this, and the evening will be doomed from the outset.

When you initiate this movie adventure, it might be a good idea to begin with a film with which you are already familiar and that you are confident about sharing with your children. This way you know how to explain the movie beforehand and create reasonable expectations. Then, your second family feature might be a movie that you have not seen, but that has a similar theme as the first, or shares the same star.

Another piece of advice applies to that first quality movie and each one thereafter: don't overload the experience with meaning. This is supposed to be entertainment, and it is absolutely essential that watching these movies be as positive and enjoyable as possible. Here are some practical guidelines that can help you make this happen:

Never present movie watching as strictly a learning experience. Every movie is a learning experience of one kind or another, but it is far better to let the "education" just happen, or emerge through casual discussion of the movie after it is over, than to build it up as a "chance to learn." You are watching these movies first and foremost because everyone's going to have a great time. You don't want to paint them as the media equivalent of brussels sprouts.

Be confident. For the most part, the movies discussed in this book are legitimately great movies. They have stood the test of time, been successful at the box office, and/or won numerous awards. It is natural for parents to want to expose their children to quality movies, just as they want to give them the best of anything. Therefore, parents who encourage their children to watch these movies can take confidence from the fact that they are acting on their best instincts and doing the right thing for their families.

Tastes differ. There's no way that every member of your family will like every movie mentioned in this book. And that's perfectly okay. The experts are sometimes wrong. Some past Oscar winners, for example, now seem to be real turkeys. Part of your confidence factor in introducing children to quality classic and contemporary movies comes from your ability to sense when the act of viewing is becoming a negative experience and having the courage to turn the VCR off. You can try again some other time with some other movie.

Be flexible in your viewing habits. You might consider, for example, watching part of a movie one weekend evening and the remainder late the next afternoon or watching a movie on successive evenings in the summer. The point is not to overload the family. If the children know they only have to watch this "great" movie for an hour, they will likely be more amenable to the experience – especially if there's a popular current hit to follow.

Just go ahead and watch. Let the kids discover the movies "on their own." When we first installed our VCR, our initial attitude was that we were going to spend some time watching the great older movies that we hadn't seen in a while or had missed completely in the revival theaters. We told our children that they were welcome to watch with us or they could do something else on their own. Being typical children raised in a video culture, they began watching with us out of curiosity and remained out of fascination – knowing they could get up and leave the room anytime they wanted. Once they stayed through one or two, the experience came to be something they looked forward to. If you watch it, they will come.

Like you, we know some otherwise fine and reasonable adults who refuse even to consider watching a black-and-white movie. Imagine what their children's attitudes must be! Most kids today expect – even demand – that their entertainment be in living color and have trouble dealing with anything more monochromatic than a street sign.

In terms of movie watching, this attitude is unfortunate, because it effectively eliminates from consideration more than fifty years of Hollywood product and the majority of the best movies ever made. People who genuinely like movies – whatever their favorite genre or style – cannot help but sample the black-and-white classics, and within a few minutes they quickly forget the fact that this great movie is not in color.

For parents who have no problem watching black-and-white movies, here is some ammunition for dealing with objections from younger family members:

Provide some historical background. Even though color film processing has been available to Hollywood moviemakers since the mid-1930s, it was not until the mid-1960s that costs were sufficiently reduced to make it feasible for virtually every movie to be made in color. In addition, movie producers of the 1950s and 1960s, though given the option of filming in color, believed that certain kinds of subjects had more impact if they were filmed in black-and-white. As recently as 1971, director Peter Bogdanovich insisted that his monumental drama *The Last Picture Show* not be filmed in color because doing so would diminish the movie's sense of gritty realism. Other popular films of this period that were not in color for artistic reasons include: *Who's Afraid of Virginia Woolf?, Darling, Ship of Fools, Dr. Strangelove, Hud,* and *The Miracle Worker.*

Watch a surefire hit. To get youngsters over their resistance to black-and-white, show them one of the titles discussed in this book that is as close to a surefire success as you can get: a great comedy classic, like the Marx Brothers' *Duck Soup;* an exciting adventure, like *Sea Wolf;* a wartime action film, like *To Hell and Back;* a suspense yarn, like *High Noon;* or a human-interest melodrama featuring children as lead characters, like *To Kill a Mockingbird.*

Compare film styles. Another tactic for getting children to sit still for black-and-white films is to show them a color film on a specific subject and then show them a black-and-white picture with a similar story line. Examples are a boxing rags-to-riches story in *Rocky* (color) and *Somebody Up There Likes Me* (B&W), and the monstrous shark in *Jaws* (color) and the monstrous ape in *King Kong* (B&W).

Getting the Most from Video Stores

Most video retail stores succeed for the same three reasons that houses sell quickly on the real estate market: location, location, location. Video customers tend to patronize the store that is closest to them and easiest to get to. This is fine when your video needs are nothing more than renting one of the current top ten hits. But parents shopping for something to watch with their children owe it to themselves to be more creative and demanding. The following are some guidelines for selecting and working with a video store:

Well-stocked children's section. You might not always shop in this section for something to watch with your kids, but an extensive selection of children's video (known in the trade as "kidvid") indicates that the store is sensitive to this market and disposed to working with you to order new titles that will appeal to the family market. The section should include more than video versions of Saturday morning cartoons and Disney standards. It also should include top-quality story tapes, such as Rabbit Ears Video's new "We All Have Tales" series, as well as Hollywood's excellent film versions of popular children's literary classics such as *The Wizard of Oz, Treasure Island, Huckleberry Finn, Oliver Twist* (and *Oliver!*), *Ivanhoe,* and *Johnny Tremain.*

Familiarity with titles. Video store personnel should be familiar with virtually every title in the store, not just the latest hits. Their knowledge should cover the older movies – called "catalog titles" in the trade – and children's selections. Not only should they know whether or not their store carries a title, but, ideally, they also should know what ages it is recommended for and what possible objectionable content it contains. If they don't have personal knowledge of a title, they should have instant access to a reference source that will provide much of this information.

Willingness to order titles for you. If a store does not carry a specific title, store personnel should be able to readily tell you (1) whether a title is available on video, (2) whether it is currently in distribution (studios remove titles from circulation for various reasons at various times), and (3) how much it costs. If you are interested in purchasing a movie, store personnel should be willing to order it for you. Ordering individual titles requires extra paperwork, and the store's percentage of the purchase price is comparatively small, so many stores do not encourage or promote the practice. But given that they are ordering dozens of titles every month anyway, it is a comparatively painless exercise, and the store should be willing to do it for you. If not, find another video store.

Willingness to order titles for themselves. The great majority of movies discussed in this book are Hollywood standards that should already be in a video store's inventory (or among its catalog titles). If they are not, you can suggest that the store purchase some of these titles. If you can get a couple of other parents to join you in making this request, the video store should act promptly to stock them. The video editions of the older titles in this book generally cost between $15 and $30 – meaning that the video store has to realize comparatively few rentals before making its money back (at a national average of $2.50 per rental, from six to twelve rentals).

Shopping for titles. Most metropolitan areas have two dozen or more video outlets; larger areas have many times that number. Each store has a different inventory of older catalog titles. This is especially true of movies made before the early 1980s, when the video boom began. Video stores that opened at that time had to stock up quickly, and titles ordered tended to reflect the personal quirks and tastes of the owners, so you can never be sure what you'll find on the shelves in any given store. If you're looking for a specific title, call around to ask for it. Once you find the title, the extra effort will cost you, at most, a few miles of travel and the time spent "joining" the new store.

Other Sources

In addition to local video stores, parents can explore other resources to access quality movies to watch with their children.

Libraries. Many public libraries now have extensive collections of older video titles. Call around to find out which libraries in your region have the best video collections, then check them out.

Parent groups. You are not alone in your concern over what your children watch on video and what you want to watch with them. No doubt other parents are equally concerned. Try seeking out like-minded parents at existing school, religious, social, and social-action groups in your community. By networking with other parents, you can build up a core group interested in video entertainment. By using this book as your guide, parents can join together in patronizing a certain video store to secure desired titles (remembering that the more rentals a store can realize, the more likely it is to order a missing title) or building up an informal lending library within the umbrella structure of the group.

About the
Rating System

The rating system most commonly used by movie producers today, was first instituted by the Motion Picture Association of America (MPAA) in November 1968. Previously, movie content had been regulated by an industry body, the Production Code Administration (PCA), established in the 1930s and authorized to order objectionable material removed from all movies distributed in the United States. Failure to comply meant that the movies had virtually no chance of being shown in public movie theaters.

Until the 1950s, most first-run movie theaters were owned by the studios producing the movies shown there. When this practice was outlawed by antitrust legislation, the industry was powerless to prevent independent theater owners from showing films without PCA approval.

As a consequence, movies were increasingly filled with profanity, violence, and sexual material, and industry leaders feared that government or community groups might launch censorship campaigns if Hollywood did not take action first. The MPAA and its industry-supported rating system were the result. This system could not unilaterally ban objectionable material, as could the PCA, but it would apply graded letter ratings and attempt to inform the public about the nature of that content.

As it stands today, the MPAA code has five designations: G, PG, PG-13, R, and NC-17. The NC-17 rating was introduced in 1990 to replace the previous X rating, a change prompted by complaints from filmmakers that the public associated the X rating with hard-core pornography, and this unfairly tainted serious movies that might have extremely objectionable content.

A rating is awarded after a film has been viewed by a seven-member MPAA Rating Board (all members are parents), with designations decided by a majority vote. After receiving a rating, producers are free to edit a film to remove objectionable content, or they can appeal a specific rating to a twenty-two-member Rating Appeals Board, where a two-thirds majority vote can overturn a Rating Board decision (board memberships do not overlap). MPAA Ratings also apply to movie print advertising and previews, or "trailers."

MPAA Ratings

Following is a summary of how one MPAA publication defines the designations:

G: general audiences; all ages admitted. This is a film that contains nothing in theme, language, nudity and sex, or violence that would, in the view of the Rating Board, be offensive to parents whose younger children view the film. Some snippets of language may go beyond polite conversation, but they are common, everyday expressions. The violence is at a minimum, there is no nudity or sex, and no drug use is shown.

PG: parental guidance suggested; some material may not be suitable for children. This is a film that parents should examine or inquire about before letting their children view. The PG label plainly states that parents may consider some material unsuitable for their children. There may be some profanity and violence, but it is deemed generally acceptable for children under seventeen. There is no drug use or explicit sex, although there may be some sensuality and brief nudity.

PG-13: parents strongly cautioned; some material may be inappropriate for children under thirteen. PG-13 is a stern warning to parents to determine whether younger children should see a film. A PG-13 film is one that goes beyond the boundaries of the PG rating but does not quite fit within the restricted (R) category. A movie including any portrayal of drug use requires at least a PG-13 rating.

If nudity is sexually oriented, the film will generally receive an R rating. Similarly, if violence is rough or persistent, the film will receive an R rating. Any use of a harsh, sexually derived word, even as an expletive, requires at least a PG-13 rating. More than one such expletive requires an R rating, as does the use of these words in a sexual context. Films containing such content may be given a PG-13 rating if the Rating Board unanimously agrees such a rating would responsibly reflect the views of most American parents.

R: restricted; children under seventeen require an accompanying parent or adult guardian. (Age varies in some jurisdictions.) In the opinion of the Rating Board, this film contains adult material. Parents are strongly urged to find out more about it before allowing their children to accompany them. An R-rated film has adult content that may include hard language, or severe violence, nudity within sensual scenes, drug abuse, or other adult elements.

NC-17: no children under seventeen admitted. This rating declares that the Rating Board believes that this is an adult film. NC-17 does not necessarily mean "obscene or pornographic." These are legal terms reserved only for judicial decisions. An NC-17 rating may indicate severe violence, sexual content, aberrational behavior, drug abuse, or any other element that most parents would not want their children to see.

Common Objections

The most widespread parental objection to the MPAA rating system is that rating information contains virtually no indication of the *kinds* of objectionable content that a movie may contain. When the NC-17 designation was announced in September 1990, the MPAA also said that it would begin making such information concerning R-rated movies available to movie critics and theater owners.

However, this requires parents to take the initiative to contact theater management or to rely on the scant data contained in published movie reviews. In addition, the information applies only to R-rated movies, ignoring the often more ambiguous PG-13 films.

The independent Film Advisory Board (FAB) has prepared an alternative rating system that contains more detailed information on objectionable content. However, their ratings are not yet widely used or available. Each film in this book made since 1968 carries the MPAA rating designation, and every one carries the authors' own recommendation as to which age group will most appreciate the movie.

Chapter 4

For Starters:
Over 100 Movies for the
Whole Family to Enjoy

Where to begin? Especially with younger children, parents must take care that the films they share together are engaging, mutually enjoyable, and especially well done. Most parents already know of some films that meet these standards. While chapters 5 and 6 discuss movies that are less obvious choices for family enjoyment, our "For Starters" list is intended to jog memories and focus on films that are notable for their lack of objectionable content and for being especially good means of introducing young viewers to films of high quality. We have included ratings where available for all movies listed here. (Movies made before 1968 or made for television do not have ratings.)

The "For Starters" movies are listed with the reminder that not all films will appeal to all viewers. The list contains only feature-length films, and all films are in color unless otherwise noted.

We've also included a list of "Kids' Top Picks" which our sons Jake and Dan compiled, to give you some insights into movies children would recommend for other parents and children. That list can be found beginning on page 32.

■ **Absent-minded Professor, The.** 1961, B&W, 97 minutes. A college science professor (Fred MacMurray) invents a mass capable of creating its own energy, calls it "flubber," and becomes the object of a riotous bidding war involving the U.S. military and an unscrupulous businessman (Keenan Wynn).

■ **Adventures of Huckleberry Finn, The.** 1985, 105 minutes. Mark Twain's classic, called by some "the great American novel," has been filmed six times (once as a musical). The original story is sufficiently fine that all versions provide quality entertainment. Best of the lot is this greatly entertaining made-for-TV film with Patrick Day playing Huck and Samm-Art Williams as his friend Jim.

■ **Adventures of Milo and Otis, The.** 1989. 76 minutes. A splendid Japanese-produced, animated feature with thrills and adventures to please adults and children, as pooch Otis goes to the rescue of his kitten pal, Milo. Droll narration by Dudley Moore. Rated G.

■ **Adventures of Robin Hood, The.** 1938, 102 minutes. Errol Flynn and Olivia de Havilland star in the best-ever rendering of the Robin Hood legend, a spellbinding treasury of Sherwood Forest folklore. For the best sequel to the story, see *Robin and Marian* (1976, 112 minutes), which has Robin (Sean Connery) returning from the Crusades, "rescuing" Marian (Audrey Hepburn) from a convent, and staging one last grand assault on the late King Richard's dastardly brother, John. Rated PG.

■ **Adventures of Tom Sawyer, The.** 1938, 77 minutes. This durable version of the Twain classic takes an amusing, slapstick approach to Tom's adventures.

■ **Airplane!** 1980, 86 minutes. First in a series of 1980s movie parodies, this is a jolly take-off on *Airport*-style dramas, with subtle digs that will appeal to parents and broad buffoonery for the kids. Rated PG.

■ **Alice in Wonderland.** 1951, 75 minutes. Lewis Carroll's beloved fairy tale has been filmed on three other occasions, with this Disney-animated musical version far and away the best.

■ **American Tail, An.** 1986, 82 minutes. A Russian-immigrant mouse arrives in America in the late nineteenth century, is separated from his family, and must use his wits to survive in the new land. Rated G.

■ **Anne of Green Gables.** 1985, 195 minutes. Taken in by a bachelor farmer and his spinster sister in this popular story, orphan Anne (Megan Follows) grows to spirited girlhood in the bleak landscape of Canada's Prince Edward Island. Followed by *Anne of Avonlea.*

■ **Around the World in 80 Days.** 1956, 167 minutes. In this ambitious, colorful, lively adaptation of Jules Verne's adventure novel, Londoner Phileas Fogg (David Niven) bets that he can circumnavigate the globe within the allotted time. Winner of Academy Award for best picture.

■ **Back to the Future.** 1985, 116 minutes. First is best in this popular series of time-travel comedy adventures, as teenager Marty McFly (Michael J. Fox) swoops backwards to the 1950s, playing a humorous key role in nurturing romance between his parents-to-be. Rated PG.

■ **Bambi.** 1942, 69 minutes. Disney Studios' inspired mix of storytelling and educational material, with the animals' life cycles paralleling those of their forest home. Everything a nature story should be.

■ **Bear, The.** 1989, 93 minutes. A bear cub loses its mother and takes on a giant kodiak as its protector, as they go about surviving in the winter wilderness and eluding a pair of relentless hunters. This epic nature film is virtually wordless and contains remarkable (if somewhat manipulative) footage of its animal subjects. While intensely considerate of wildlife, the film contains some brief scenes of human-to-animal violence. Rated PG.

■ **Bedknobs and Broomsticks.** 1971, 117 minutes. Angela Lansbury plays an apprentice witch in an English seacoast town at the start of World War II, using her supernatural powers to entertain youngsters and fight would-be Nazi invaders. An inspired mix of live action, animation, and musical numbers. Rated G.

■ **Benji.** 1974, 86 minutes. A talented orphan dog outsmarts a gang of kidnappers who snatch two young children. Followed by several sequels. Rated G.

■ **Black Stallion, The.** 1979, 118 minutes. A boy and his wild horse survive a shipwreck to become a champion racing team, with a boost from trainer Mickey Rooney. Rated G.

■ **Born Free.** 1966, 96 minutes. Husband-and-wife game wardens in Kenya adopt a lion cub, raise her to adulthood, and then must set her free. Heart-warming classic of endearing simplicity.

■ **Boy Named Charlie Brown, A.** 1969, 85 minutes. The first and best film featuring the Peanuts' comic strip characters, climaxing with Charlie's entry in a spelling bee. Rated G.

■ **Brave Little Toaster, The.** 1987, 96 minutes. A plucky toaster named Slots leads four other anthropomorphized appliances abandoned in a mountain cabin on a search for their master in the big city. Clever story and catchy songs add to the animated fun.

■ **Brave One, The.** 1956, 100 minutes. A Mexican farm boy becomes overly attached to a pet calf being raised for the bullfight ring and tries valiantly to prevent it from having to enter the arena. (Note to parents: While the bull, Gitano, has a few frightening moments in his bout with the matador, he escapes injury.)

■ **Bridge On the River Kwai, The.** 1957, 161 minutes. An ideal action-adventure film for the whole family set in a tropical Japanese prisoner-of-war camp during World War II. Parents can appreciate the subtle battle of wits between the British POWs and their Japanese captors, while the children will relish efforts by American guerrillas to blow up the bridge. Winner of Oscars for best picture and best actor (Alec Guinness).

■ **Butch Cassidy and the Sundance Kid.** 1969, 112 minutes. Two legendary outlaws are given a delightful comic turn, as stand-ins Paul Newman and Robert Redford rob trains, elude a relentless posse ("Who *are* those guys?"), and flee to South America to continue their escapades. Rated PG.

■ **Cat Ballou.** 1965, 96 minutes. This frothy, comical Western, with occasional musical interludes, has school-marm Jane Fonda turning outlaw to avenge her father's death and hiring a notorious gun-slinger (Lee Marvin in an Oscar winning role) to help her out.

■ **Cat From Outer Space, The.** 1978, 104 minutes. An alien tabby needs help from earthling scientists to help repair its spaceship and return home, with whimsical spy shenanigans delaying the process. Rated G.

■ **Cinderella.** 1950, 75 minutes. Another Disney classic, with the familiar fairy tale greatly embellished by outstanding animation, humorous minor characters, and original tunes.

■ **Charlotte's Web.** 1973, 85 minutes. Delightful animation of E.B. White's barnyard tale of a runt pig who becomes famous and wins awards with the help of a super-spelling spider. Rated G.

■ **Christmas Carol, A.** 1984, 100 minutes. Colorful and riveting made-for-TV version of Dickens's story features George C. Scott, in one of his best performances, as Ebeneezer Scrooge. A highly-regarded black-and-white film version was produced in England in 1950 with Alastair Sim as Scrooge.

■ **Cloak and Dagger.** 1984, 101 minutes. This sleeper surprise picture works wonderfully as an espionage suspense story and a childhood fantasy tale. A youngster with a lively imagination (Henry Thomas) becomes embroiled in a real spy caper and imagines his make-believe superhero Jack Flash (Dabney Coleman, who also plays his dad) will come to his rescue. Rated PG.

■ **Cross Creek.** 1983, 122 minutes. Children's book author Marjorie Kinnan Rawlings moves from New York City to rural Florida and gets to know some of the locals who will later become characters in her works such as *The Yearling.* Rated PG.

■ **Empire Strikes Back, The.** 1980, 124 minutes. The almost-as-good sequel to *Star Wars* (see page 30) has Luke Skywalker (Mark Hamill) learning about life from the unlikely guru Yoda. Rated PG.

■ **Fantasia.** 1940, 120 minutes. This is probably Disney's most popular work for adults and children, adapting spirited animated stories to eight different works of classical music, including the beloved *Sorcerer's Apprentice* featuring Mickey Mouse and the dancing brooms.

■ **Father of the Bride.** 1950, B&W/colorized, 93 minutes. A quick-paced comedy of mid-century American suburban culture, as doting father Spencer Tracy presides over the hectic wedding preparations for daughter Elizabeth Taylor. (Not to be confused with the 1991 remake.)

■ **Field of Dreams.** 1989, 106 minutes. An Iowa farmer (Kevin Costner) heeds a voice telling him to build a perfect baseball diamond out in his cornfield so that deceased players can return for one last time at bat. Evocative, moving fantasy about following your dreams. Rated PG.

■ **Five Thousand Fingers of Doctor T, The.** 1958, 88 minutes. The ultimate, unwilling piano student's nightmare has young Bart Collins (Tommy Rettig) dreaming of a prison-like institution where small boys are tyrannized by a mad music teacher (Hans Conreid). Script co-authored by Dr. Seuss.

■ **Flight of the Navigator, The.** 1986, 90 minutes. A twelve-year-old boy returns to earth after an eight-year UFO trip and finds, although he has not aged a day, life is appreciably different. Skillful, intelligent mix of sci-fi, drama, and humor. Rated PG.

■ **400 Blows, The.** 1959, B&W, 99 minutes. A young Parisian boy at odds with his parents, teachers, and most of his classmates battles for a sense of identity and self-esteem. Directed by French master Francois Truffaut. In French, with English subtitles, but easily accessible to all.

■ **Funny Thing Happened on the Way to the Forum, A.** 1966, 99 minutes. This rambunctious musical set in early Rome has broad humor, colorful characters, and lively tunes to appeal to all ages. Zero Mostel and Phil Silvers star.

■ **Girl Who Spelled Freedom, The.** 1986, 100 minutes. An affecting, made-for-TV drama of a Cambodian refugee child (Kieu Chinh) who arrives in the U.S.

without knowing any English and within a few short years wins a national spelling contest.

■ **Glory.** 1989, 122 minutes. An inspiring story of the first black regiment to fight in the Union Army during the Civil War and the idealistic white officer (Matthew Broderick) who leads the men. The movie's powerful drama and important message far outweigh the mild profanity and brief, believable scenes of battlefield violence that earn it a dubious R rating.

■ **Great Escape, The.** 1963, 168 minutes. American and English POWs concoct an intricate plan to escape from a German prison camp in World War II in an intelligent, frequently humorous adventure story that will have adults and children on the edges of their seats. Outstanding cast includes James Garner, Steve McQueen, and James Coburn.

■ **Great Muppet Caper, The.** 1981, 95 minutes. The second of Jim Henson's sublime Muppet pictures has the puppet posse in London trying to solve the theft of the fabled jewel, the Baseball Diamond. Includes Miss Piggy's wonderful tribute to Esther Williams's movies. Rated G.

■ **Hans Christian Anderson.** 1952, 120 minutes. This musical fantasy "inspired by" the life of the Danish storyteller is especially memorable for its impressive ballet sequences, featuring the French ballerina Jeanmaire.

■ **Harvey.** 1950, B&W, 104 minutes. The nicest man ever portrayed on film, friendly-to-a-fault Elwood P. Dowd (James Stewart) tries to elude those who would put him in an institution while sharing a few jokes on the world with his pal, a six-foot-three-inch invisible rabbit. Sheer heaven.

■ **Heaven Can Wait.** 1978, 100 minutes. An amiable comedy in which professional football quarterback (Warren Beatty) is mistakenly called to heaven before his time and then must find a suitable body to inhabit in order to return to earth. Rated PG.

■ **Heidi.** Johanna Spyri's story of a Swiss girl forced to leave her cozy home in the Alps for the sometimes cruel world of the city is available in three video versions, each worthy of viewing: 1) 1937, B&W/colorized, 88-minute, starring Shirley Temple; 2) 1965, 95-minute, made in Austria; 3) 1968, 110 minutes, made-for-TV, with Maximilian Schell, Jean Simmons, and Jennifer Edwards (as Heidi).

■ **Honey, I Shrunk the Kids.** 1989, 93 minutes. Dad Rick Moranis is a crazed, attic inventor whose kids accidentally trip off one of his latest creations – a miniaturization ray – and are reduced to ant size. A grand special-effects comedy. Rated PG.

■ **Hoosiers.** 1986, 114 minutes. An inspiring story of sportsmanship and grit, as hard-working, tough-talking high school basketball coach Gene Hackman helps his small town, midwest team deal with off-court problems and on-court challenges on their way to an upset victory in the 1951 state championships. Rated PG.

■ **Incredible Journey, The.** 1963, 80 minutes. Three household pets – two dogs and a cat – think they've been abandoned (someone is actually taking care of them in their owners' absence) and set across Canada to return home.

■ **It's a Mad, Mad, Mad, Mad World.** 1963, 175 minutes. Virtually every comedian of note from the 1950s and early '60s pops up in this epic screen comedy, all of them searching (madly) for hidden bank loot.

■ **It's a Wonderful Life.** 1946, B&W/colorized, 129 minutes. Everyone's favorite American Christmas tale can never be seen too many times (and is even better seen without the commercial interruptions that plague TV showings).

■ **Johnny Tremain.** 1957, 80 minutes. An apprentice silversmith in Boston in the 1770s joins the Sons of Liberty and becomes embroiled in the events leading up to "the shot heard 'round the world" at the Battle of Lexington.

■ **Journey of Natty Gann, The.** 1985, 101 minutes. A depression-era saga of a young girl (Meredith Salenger) who disguises herself as a boy and travels from Chicago to the West Coast to be reunited with her father, with a wild wolf joining her as pet/protector. Rated PG.

■ **Journey to the Center of the Earth.** 1959, 132 minutes. This well-done sci-fi adventure of a group of explorers penetrating to the earth's core is based on Jules Verne's novel.

■ **Jungle Book, The.** 1967, 78 minutes. This animated musical loosely adapted from Rudyard Kipling's Mowgli stories of a boy raised by wolves was the last film in which Walt Disney was personally involved.

■ **King and I, The.** 1956, 133 minutes. An English governess (Deborah Kerr) arrives at the court of the King of Siam (Yul Brynner) to tutor his large brood of children including an uppity heir apparent. A timeless musical with lovely performances by Kerr and Brynner.

■ **Lady and the Tramp, The.** 1955, 75 minutes. Ne'er-do-well hound befriends an uppity society pooch in an enchanting animated Disney musical that will appeal to adults as a whimsical parable and to children as a lovely fairytale romance.

■ **Lassie Come Home.** 1943, 88 minutes. Impoverished British family is forced to sell their beloved pet collie, only to have the dog leave her new owners and make her tortuous way back "home." All-time tearjerker will have adults and children alike reaching for the tissues.

■ **Lion, the Witch and the Wardrobe, The.** 1979, 95 minutes. An old wardrobe provides the way into a lively fantasy world for four young children in an animated film based on C.S. Lewis's *Chronicles of Narnia.*

■ **Little Mermaid, The.** 1989, 76 minutes. Ariel, an aquatic nymph, is tempted to turn human in order to have the man of her dreams in a popular musical animated tale that many think is better than anything Disney Studios produced in the 1940s and '50s. Rated G.

■ **Little Miss Marker.** 1934, B&W, 80 minutes. This outstanding Shirley Temple vehicle has the enormously popular child star "won" as a gambling debt by a crusty racetrack bettor (Adolphe Menjou) and then proceeding to reform the hard-bitten betting crowd.

■ **Longest Day, The.** 1962, B&W, 180 minutes. A remarkable achievement in historical movie-making, with the story of the epochal D-Day landing of 1944 told in a seamless string of stirring vignettes (from the German and Allied sides). Features dozens of major stars in cameo performances with impressively little violence or bloodshed for a "war" movie.

■ **Love Bug, The.** 1969, 107 minutes. Disney live-action picture features a Volkswagen with a distinctive personality. Falls into the silly, fun-for-all category. Followed by several *Herbie* sequels.

■ **Man Who Knew Too Much, The.** 1956, 120 minutes. Great family introduction to the work of suspense master Alfred Hitchcock. A young boy (Christopher Olsen) is kidnapped and his parents (James Stewart, Doris Day) comb the back streets of London searching for him.

■ **Man Who Would Be King, The.** 1975, 129 minutes. Classic Rudyard Kipling story of two British soldiers who hike into a remote Himalayan kingdom and try to swindle the natives out of their gold and jewels. A top-rank action adventure with Sean Connery and Michael Caine in peak form. Rated PG.

■ **Mary Poppins.** 1964, 140 minutes. One of those rare movies where everything works to perfection and few can resist its substantial charms. Julie Andrews and Dick Van Dyck star.

■ **Midsummer Night's Dream, A.** 1935, 117 minutes. A painless and entertaining introduction to Shakespeare – Hollywood style – as parents will find, with James Cagney as Bottom and Mickey Rooney as Puck.

■ **Miracle on 34th Street.** 1947, B&W/colorized, 96 minutes. A department store Santa Claus (Edmund Gwenn) goes on "trial" to prove to a disbelieving child (Natalie Wood) that St. Nick is for real.

■ **Mister Roberts.** 1955, 123 minutes. A warm, witty, achingly human comedy-drama of daily routine on a cargo ship during World War II, with brilliant performances by Henry Fonda, James Cagney, and Jack Lemmon. Try it and you'll never regret it.

■ **Moby Dick.** 1956, 116 minutes. Herman Melville's story of Captain Ahab (Gregory Peck) and his obsessive hunt for a great white whale is faithfully captured in this ambitious film version.

■ **Monty Python and the Holy Grail.** 1975, 90 minutes. Granted, the Python troupe's humor is an acquired taste, but once it's acquired, it's a lifelong addiction! And this, fans contend, is the best vehicle with which to test your taste buds. (Note: A couple of bloody, if funny, scenes.) Rated PG.

■ **Muppet Movie, The.** 1979, 94 minutes. The Muppet gang's film premier has Kermit leaving his Georgia swamp home and heading, appropriately, to Hollywood. Rated G.

■ **Music Man, The.** 1962, 151 minutes. A high-octane musical about fast-talking instrument salesman Harold Hill (Robert Preston) and his effort to get the townspeople of River City, Iowa, to buy his wares to start a youth band.

■ **My Fair Lady.** 1964, 170 minutes. Speech professor Henry Higgins (Rex Harrison), on a bet, plucks cockney lass Eliza Doolittle (Audrey Hepburn) from the London streets and transforms her into a society belle. One of the great musicals.

■ **National Velvet.** 1944, 125 minutes. A winning film about a young British girl (Elizabeth Taylor) determined to ride her horse to victory in the Grand National Steeplechase. Child-star Taylor's breakthrough film.

■ **Natural, The.** 1984, 134 minutes. Of all the many baseball movies, this is the best for evoking the sheer luminescent magic of the game, with Robert Redford playing out-of-nowhere superstar Roy Hobbs. Rated PG.

■ **Never Cry Wolf.** 1983, 105 minutes. Canadian wildlife author Farley Mowat (Charles Martin Smith) goes into the Arctic wilderness to study wolves and learns to survive in rugged terrain. Rated PG.

■ **Nutty Professor, The.** 1963, 107 minutes. Considered to be the funniest comedy from popular film and TV cut-up Jerry Lewis, with the star featured as a nerdy science professor who creates a magic potion that transforms him into a suave lady's man.

■ **Oliver!** 1968, 153 minutes. The Oscar-winning musical version of Charles Dickens's novel, featuring devious Mr. Fagin (Ron Moody) and his school for young pick-pockets in the London slums. Rated G.

■ **Old Yeller.** 1957, 83 minutes. A classic boy-meets-dog family melodrama, set in Texas in the 1850s.

■ **On Golden Pond.** 1981, 109 minutes. This is best known as a star vehicle for Katherine Hepburn, Henry Fonda and Jane Fonda, but the most affecting relationship in this comic-drama of family bonds is that of Jane Fonda's son (Doug McKeon) with his grandparents. Rated PG.

■ **Operation Petticoat.** 1959, 124 minutes. Highly recommended, this goofy, happy comedy has two officers (Cary Grant, Tony Curtis) trying to restore their crippled submarine to sea duty during World War II.

■ **Paper Moon.** 1973, B&W, 102 minutes. Depression-era con man Ryan O'Neil takes on a young sidekick (played by his real-life daughter Tatum), who soon becomes the better swindler of the two. First-rate entertainment, with some classic moments of Tatum outsmarting her elders. Rated PG.

■ **Parent Trap, The.** 1961, 124 minutes. Haley Mills plays both parts as a set of twin girls reunited at a summer camp, conspiring to get their divorced parents back together.

■ **Peter Pan.** 1953, 77 minutes. Yet another animated musical classic from Disney studios.

■ **Pinocchio.** 1940, 87 minutes. And another (and this one has "When You Wish Upon A Star"!).

■ **Places in the Heart.** 1984, 102 minutes. Newly widowed Sally Field and her children struggle to keep the family cotton farm, with the help of a couple of social cast-offs – blind border John Malkovich and black laborer Danny Glover. Rated PG.

■ **Prancer.** 1989, 102 minutes. The best, recent, instant "Christmas classic," has the daughter (Rebecca Harrell) of a financially troubled midwestern farmer (Sam Elliot) nursing a crippled reindeer back to health, believing it is one of Santa's own. Rated G.

■ **Princess Bride, The.** 1987, 98 minutes. A lovely updating of the fairy tale genre, courtesy of director Rob Reiner, with great swashbuckling scenes mixed in with amusing (especially for adults) comic bits by Billy Crystal, Christopher Guest, and Peter Falk. Rated PG.

■ **Raiders of the Lost Ark.** 1981, 115 minutes. The first of the Indiana Jones adventures has Indy fighting to keep the original Ten Commandments tablets from falling into the hands of Nazi thugs. Contains some scenes of bloodshed and lots of rough-housing. Rated PG.

■ **Railway Children, The.** 1972, 102 minutes. A comic drama, set in 1905, in which a family of British kids conspires to clear their father of a false criminal charge. Rated G.

■ **Return of the Jedi, The.** 1983, 133 minutes. The last of the *Star Wars* trilogy maintains the series' remarkable quality. Rated PG.

■ **Rio Bravo.** 1959, 141 minutes. A dandy, good-time Western with many laughs, good action, appealing characters and even a tune or two. Stars John Wayne as a sheriff trying to hold on to a valuable prisoner, with help from deputies Dean Martin, Ricky Nelson, and Walter Brennan.

■ **Rocky.** 1976, 119 minutes. What's this – a Sylvester Stallone boxing movie in a list of family pictures? You betcha! The first Rocky is a wonderfully warm, nice-guys-finish-first story, has a sweetly affecting romance thrown in, and the pugilistic mayhem is minimal. Bill Conti's rousing score alone makes the experience unforgettable. Rated PG.

■ **Sarah, Plain and Tall.** 1992, 98 minutes. The two children of a widowed farmer (Christopher Walken) on the Kansas prairie in about 1910 cautiously appraise the mail-order bride (Glenn Close) their father has invited from the East to join them to "make a difference" in their lives. Made for TV.

■ **Sea Hawk.** 1940, B&W/colorized, 127 minutes. Errol Flynn in one of his classic "swashbuckler roles," playing a character based on the heroics of Sir Francis Drake in organizing a British guerrilla fleet (the Sea Hawks) to frustrate Spain's efforts to dominate the world's seas with its mighty Armada. Superior historical action-drama.

■ **Secret of NIMH, The.** 1982, 82 minutes. The first feature from Don Bluth Studios offers a sly, government satire in presenting a breed of superintelligent rats, courtesy of the National Institute of Mental Health. Rated G.

■ **Shenandoah.** 1965, 105 minutes. An independent-minded Virginia farmer (James Stewart) tries to remain aloof from the Civil War, until Confederate agents try to draft his sons and one boy is captured by Union soldiers. Moving family drama; powerful anti-war statement.

■ **Sleeping Beauty.** 1959, 75 minutes. A lavish Disney rendition of the popular fairy tale, with score by Tchaikovsky.

■ **So Dear To My Heart.** 1948, 84 minutes. This lesser known Disney live-action feature (with some animated sequences) is one of the best and should be "must" family viewing. It recreates a turn-of-the-century world of civility and decency while telling of a boy (Bobby Driscoll) determined to enter his homely black lamb in a state fair contest.

■ **Sound of Music, The.** 1965, 174 minutes. Julie Andrews and a gaggle of button-cute kids escape from the Nazis, singing all the way. Irresistible fun.

■ **Stand and Deliver.** 1987, 105 minutes. Los Angeles high school math teacher (Edward James Olmos) inspires his poor, Hispanic students to excel in calculus, winning top grades in a national Advanced Placement test. Rated PG.

■ **Star Wars.** 1977, 121 minutes. Why is this the best-ever sci-fi adventure movie? Because, for all the whiz-bang special effects, it is still about three attractive and very human beings: Luke Skywalker (Mark Hammil), Princess Leia (Carrie Fisher) and Han Solo (Harrison Ford). And one wookie. Rated PG.

■ **Swiss Family Robinson, The.** 1960, 128 minutes. This picturesque, lively retelling of the familiar tale of a marooned family building an island paradise will appeal to children as a great adventure yarn and to adults as a wistful fantasy.

■ **Superman.** 1978, 143 minutes. The most super of comic-book superheroes is the inspiration for the best superhero movie yet, with Christopher Reeve as the Man of Steel. Rated PG.

■ **That Darn Cat.** 1965, 116 minutes. A supersmart tabby leads FBI agent Dean Jones on the track of kidnappers in a jolly Disney comedy.

■ **That's Entertainment.** 1974, color and B&W, 132 minutes. This anthology of highlights from the great MGM movie musicals of the 1930s, '40s and '50s is the ideal way to introduce youngsters to this kind of delightful entertainment (and for adults to recapture some memories). Next you can target some titles for full-length viewing. Rated G.

■ **Treasure Island.** 1990, 132 minutes. The most recent version of Robert Louis Stevenson's spine-tingling adventure novel is impressive entertainment, shot on location in the Caribbean, and featuring Charlton Heston as the snarly Long John Silver and Christian Bale (*Empire of the Sun*) as Jim Hawkins. Earlier versions are also highly recommended: 1934, 105 minutes, B&W/colorized, with Wallace Beery and Jackie Cooper; 1950, 96 minutes, with Robert Newton and Bobby Driscoll.

■ **20,000 Leagues Under the Sea.** 1954, 127 minutes. Kirk Douglas stars in this rip-snorting rendition of the Jules Verne sci-fi novel with its terrific special effects, including a giant squid that terrorizes Captain Nemo's futuristic submarine.

■ **Wee Willie Winkie.** 1937, B&W, 100 minutes. This is one of Shirley Temple's best and most exotic films, with the moppet going to live with a crusty old uncle (C. Aubrey Smith) at a British army outpost in colonial India.

■ **Where the Red Fern Grows.** 1974, 90 minutes. Parents and children who like dogs – real dogs – will enjoy this story of a boy in Depression-era Oklahoma who learns about commitment and responsibility while caring for the family's two hunting dogs. Rated G.

■ **White Fang.** 1990, 107 minutes. An exciting Jack London adventure, with young man (Ethan Hawke) going into the Alaskan wilderness during the Yukon gold rush to look for his deceased father's claim, and befriending the wild dog of the title. Rated PG.

■ **Who Framed Roger Rabbit.** 1988, 103 minutes. A spectacularly inventive mix of live and animated action, so chockful of detail you need several viewings to catch it all.

■ **Wind in the Willows, The.** 1949, 75 minutes. This brief animated adaptation of Kenneth Grahame's timeless tale of J. Thaddeus Toad & Friends is generally regarded as one of Disney's finest efforts.

■ **Wizard of Oz, The.** 1939, 119 minutes. Maybe no parent needs to be reminded of the Dorothy and Toto show, but maybe you do need to be reminded to see it again . . . and again.

■ **Yearling, The.** 1946, 128 minutes. The sensitive, lovingly produced story of a boy in rural Florida who becomes attached to a young deer. Based on the novel by Marjorie Kinnan Rawlings (see *Cross Creek,* above).

Kids' Top Picks: Jake and Dan's List

We asked our sons Jacob (age 17) and Daniel (age 13) to reflect on their past seven years of movie-watching and draw up a list of favorite films that they would enthusiastically encourage other children to get their families to watch. Here, in their own words, are their choices. Except where noted, these films contain no objectionable content.

■ **Breaking Away.** 1979, color, 100 minutes. Fun growing-up comedy that is also very inspiring. Everyone will want to take up bicycling the next day! Rated PG.

■ **Bridge on the River Kwai.** 1957, color, 161 minutes. Fantastic movie – great story, great characters. Also, one of the most suspenseful endings you'll ever see on film. An exciting, edge-of-your-seat picture.

■ **Butch Cassidy and the Sundance Kid.** 1969, color, 112 minutes. One of those Westerns that is so easy to get caught up in that you find yourself cheering for the "bad guys." (Rated PG; contains minimal gunplay and a modest bedroom scene.)

■ **Duck Soup.** 1933, B&W, 70 minutes. One of the funniest movies in existence. The Marx Brothers at their best.

■ **Field of Dreams.** 1989, color, 106 minutes. A movie for baseball-lovers and non-baseball-lovers alike. It's really about people following what's in their hearts. Kevin Costner's best. You can't see it too many times. Rated PG.

■ **Great Escape, The.** 1963, color, 168 minutes. One of the most exciting and complete World War II prisoners-of-war movies. The prisoners' preparations and the escape itself provide great drama.

■ **Never Cry Wolf.** 1983, color, 105 minutes. Beautiful scenery and wonderful story of a man surviving in remote wilderness. (Rated PG; the hero runs through the snow naked.)

■ **On the Waterfront.** 1954, B&W, 108 minutes. Impossible to say how good a movie it is! Incredibly compelling drama. Many reasons to see it, including being able to quote Marlon Brando's I-coulda-been-a-contender taxi-cab scene. (Note: Unrated, but contains a brutal-but-dramatic beating scene.)

■ **To Kill a Mockingbird.** 1962, B&W, 129 minutes. A must-see for everyone in America. Gregory Peck's Atticus Finch is one of the nicest and most likeable screen characters ever. Also one of the bravest.

■ **Topper.** 1937, B&W, 97 minutes. One of Cary Grant's best and easily one of the funniest ghost movies ever.

■ **Yankee Doodle Dandy.** 1942, B&W, 126 minutes. You'll all be able to sing along with most of the songs, even if you have never heard of George M. Cohan. That's how successful a songwriter he was! The movie's energy is inescapable.

■ **Yellow Submarine.** 1968, color, 85 minutes. Who ever thought up the idea of the Beatles as animated characters was a genius. Perfect combination of great Beatles' music, amazing animation, and funny one-liners.

Chapter 5

A Closer Look: Popular Themes in Some Important Movies

This chapter is organized around fifteen popular movie themes that also relate to events, trends, and phenomena in the world around us. Some of these themes are very serious (such as courtroom dramas), others are whimsical (such as movies about monsters and aliens), while most fall somewhere in between (such as movies about rebellious youth).

Our objective with this chapter is to highlight quality movies that may not readily be thought of as family-viewing fare, as well as to point out features of the films that might be grist for family conversations once a movie is finished. All of the films discussed in this chapter are also described, in alphabetized capsule review form, in chapter 6. Readers are urged to turn to chapter 6 for additional rating and content information, before deciding on a film's suitability for your family.

Classic Comedy

There is no better way to interest young people in the great movies of the past than by having them watch one of the classic comedies. Introducing a youngster – or anyone – to his or her first Marx Brothers movie, for example, remains one of life's great sharing experiences, to be treasured across the generations. Even in these jaded times, nothing quite prepares a person for Chico, Harpo, and Groucho and the kind of fantasy world where Rufus T. Firefly can lead nations.

Of course, there aren't many subjects that can start an argument faster than the question of what's funny and what's not or who's funny and who's not. But several exceptional movie comedies are generally considered to be true classics, time-less and beyond controversy, and some of these are singled out here.

Comedies That Have Aged the Best

The first group of comedies we will discuss were released in the years 1933 to 1944, an era that stands as a golden age of movie comedy. This period is remarkable for its abundance of performing, writing, and directing talents, for the quality and quantity of fine films released, and for the headlong energy that the best of these films exude. Even today, pictures such as *Duck Soup, The Awful Truth, The Philadelphia Story,* and *Woman of the Year* still throw off enough energy to power their own galaxies.

What made this period so special? This was the time of the Great Depression and the darkest days of Nazism, Pearl Harbor, and World War II. Perhaps it was just another case of hard times begetting great escapist entertainment. Or it might be that the arrival of talking pictures in the late 1920s unleashed pent-up comic talents that had found limited outlet in silent movies.

The films presented here are among the comedies that have aged the best and appeal to the widest contemporary audience. They are, above all, very stylish films, as even Marx Brothers' lunacies were executed with rarefied wit and elegant staging. And they are films undertaken with a devotion and caring for comic craft that is remarkable in a day when monosyllabic vulgarities and violent car crashes attempt to pass for film humor.

Generally considered the most polished of the Marx Brothers' thirteen pictures, *Duck Soup* (1933) has the brothers leading the plucky little nation of Freedonia into battle against archenemy Sylvania and contains perhaps their most famous bit of comic business: the Groucho-Harpo mirror scene. A close runner-up among Marx fans is *A Night At the Opera* (1935), with the brothers running amok in the world of high culture and a tolerable Kitty Carlisle-Allan Jones romance interwoven with the classic comedy sequences (including the familiar scene in a very overcrowded ocean-liner bedroom).

Charles Chaplin contributed enough fine films and timeless comic moments to deserve whole books devoted to his art. His 1936 film *Modern Times* is a grand collection of Chaplinesque comic inventions and physical bumbles that will interest young viewers and continue to impress adults with its subtlety and wit.

A silent movie in the talkie era, *Modern Times* follows Chaplin as he loses his factory job and makes common cause with a street waif (Paulette Goddard) to create a small island of sanity in a world gone slightly mad. Included is the often anthologized scene in which overly obsessive assembly-line worker Chaplin lands on a conveyor belt, gets carried into a huge machine, and is run (unharmed) through a series of enormous gears and belts.

From his earlier career, Chaplin's most famous silent era picture was 1925's *The Gold Rush*, which finds his fabled Little Tramp character in Alaska during the Yukon gold rush and suffering all manner of cruel, if amusing, fates (includes the famous scene in which the destitute Tramp is reduced to eating his shoes).

Cary Grant may not have invented the so-called screwball comedy, but he did provide its definitive on-screen interpretation. In *Topper* (1937), for example, Grant and spouse Constance Bennett return to life as wacky ghosts after their untimely demise in an auto accident. They decide to spend their hereafter days livening up the life of their stuffy banker friend Cosmo Topper (Roland Young), who alone can "see" his departed friends.

Even better is *The Awful Truth* (1937), in which divorcing socialites Grant and Irene Dunne spend so much time trying to sabotage each other's future independence that they come to realize they simply can't live without each other. This film has a buoyant spirit and brisk dialogue that keep us suspended in wondrous amusement for the duration. This is as good as screwball comedy gets.

Grant is but one of the factors at work in *The Philadelphia Story* (1940), a grandly elegant, wonderfully fast-paced delight that costars the equally spectacular Katharine Hepburn and James Stewart (who won an Oscar for his work here). It's all about Hepburn ditching Grant for a new hubby, falling fleetingly in love with Stewart, and then falling back in love with Grant. This is all told within the context of a whirlwind few days at the Hepburn character's family estate on Philadelphia's Main Line.

The Philadelphia Story is a triumphant film that is gloriously greater than the sum of its parts, but the most important of those parts remain Grant, Stewart, and Hepburn. Rarely have we seen ensemble acting of such seamless grace and pinpoint perfection. That the script also contains pleasantly instructive notes on the ethics of interpersonal relations is all the better.

After her exceptional turn with Grant and Stewart in *The Philadelphia Story* — before which time she had been labeled "box office poison" by Hollywood moguls — Hepburn hooked up with Spencer Tracy, previously known as a straight dramatic actor, and made the first of their great screen comedies together, *Woman of the Year* (1942). Hepburn is a celebrated international political columnist and Tracy an earthy sportswriter, and theirs' is a classic comic romance that is the stuff of movie legend.

Hepburn and Tracy were to be costars for the next thirty-five years, making some of the screen's brightest comedies. Among their films mentioned elsewhere in this book are *State of the Union* (1948), listed with other films commenting on the political scene; *Adam's Rib* (1949), discussed with other courtroom dramas; and (though not a comedy), *Guess Who's Coming To Dinner* (1967), included with films on race relations. The Hepburn-Tracy chemistry was based on a superficial clash of personalities, buoyed by an underlying gruff decency and emotional dependency.

Preston Sturges, one of Hollywood's most intelligent comedy masters, was a gifted writer of clever, literate scripts and a director who manipulated screen relationships like a police officer handles rush-hour traffic. Sturges made pinball comedies – swank, snappy, glitzy, and noisy – with the on-screen action always in breathtaking motion.

One of his finest films was *The Miracle of Morgan's Creek* (1944), which finds patriotic Morgan Creek maiden Trudy Kockenlocker (Betty Hutton) unable to remember who made her pregnant after an all-night party at a nearby Army base, and still finding true love with her townie suitor Norvil (Eddie Bracken). When Trudy and Norvil attempt to sneak away and take out a marriage license under the names of "Mr. and Mrs. Ratzkeywatsky," the scene is a howler.

(Viewing hint: To help your children understand the ending of *The Miracle of Morgan's Creek*, you might explain the phenomenon of the Dionne quintuplets, five infants born in Canada in 1934 who were the first quintuplets in recorded medical history to survive into childhood and who became international celebrities in the process.)

A second recommended Sturges feature, *Hail the Conquering Hero* (1944), makes jolly fun of our cozy notions about war heroes – a typically audacious topic for Sturges to tackle at the height of the patriotic drum-beating of World War II. The "hero" is well-meaning Woody Truesmith (Eddie Bracken), who, having received a medical discharge from the Marines, is unable to face his mother (widow of an authentic World War I hero) and agrees to go along with a ruse concocted by some overly friendly Marine buddies. Typical of Sturges comedies, events get out of hand, and soon "heroic" Woody is treated to a hometown parade and drafted to run for mayor. Sturges uses Woody's madcap experience as an opportunity to examine American values, and, as with most of his work, the satirical points still ring true. (Sturges's 1941 film *Sullivan's Travels* is discussed in our section on movies about show business.)

Following its golden age of comedy, Hollywood's comic sensibility suddenly went haywire. In part this was due to outside influences: postwar cultural pretentiousness, Communist witch-hunts, and television's preemption of much comic territory with the weekly craziness of "I Love Lucy" and Milton Berle's "Texaco Star Theater." Although circumstances have changed today, the state of comedy on the whole has not. What has been in especially short supply since comedy's golden age is the kind of inspired slapstick comedies that appeal to youngsters and adults alike with their anarchic charm. The following films are exceptions to this trend, and are notable for containing elements of surprise, innovation, and imagination worthy of their classic golden age predecessors.

The best of the great Billy Wilder's comedies, *Some Like It Hot* (1959), is set in 1930s Chicago and has Tony Curtis and Jack Lemmon as unwitting witnesses to the infamous St. Valentine's Day massacre. The pair dress up as women so they can masquerade as members of an all-girl jazz band and thus escape Chicago and the gangland hit men out to get them. (Marilyn Monroe does an appealing turn as the group's vocalist.) What makes the comedy work is that Curtis and Lemmon play their parts plumb-line straight, steering the movie away from cheap and predictable gimmickry and helping to produce a highly polished piece of filmmaking.

Vintage Mel Brooks craziness is some of the best comedy ever witnessed on-screen, and *The Producers* (1968) is his craziest of all. A down-on-his-luck Broadway show producer (Zero Mostel) enlists the aid of a timid accountant (Gene Wilder) to help him perpetrate a scam whereby wealthy widows are sweet-talked into bankrolling a play so wretched that it's doomed to fail, whereupon producers Mostel and Wilder will skip town with the ladies' dough. The show they stage is a musical called "Springtime For Hitler," and their scheme is sabotaged when the play is a huge, campy hit ("Springtime's" opening dance sequence is a classic parody of Broadway spectacles).

Another superb Brooks film, ideal for younger audiences, is *Young Frankenstein* (1974), a nutty, clever retelling of the classic monster story. Brooks's hero is the original Dr. Frankenstein's nephew (Gene Wilder), who wants to live down the family's unsavory legacy but just can't avoid getting into the monster-building business himself and reliving his uncle's mad adventures — albeit to more humorous effect. The scene in which the monster (played by Peter Boyle) debuts before a black-tie opera-house crowd must be ranked as one of the funniest passages in movie-comedy history.

Start the Revolution without Me (1970) attracted scant attention on its release but has built up a cult following in the interim and is now a staple on video store shelves. The film is set at the time of the French Revolution, with Donald Sutherland and Gene Wilder each playing a set of identical twins, who are inadvertently switched at birth. So we have one Sutherland-Wilder pair raised as highborn gentry, the other as poor peasants; one pro-monarchy, the other active revolutionaries. Later in life, their paths cross, they are mistaken for each other, and they wind up in the wrong fights on the wrong sides. The movie's success lies in its being able to keep the confused-identity business bounding along with a keen sense of style and in the actors' ability to keep their characters fresh and consistently funny.

In a more perfect world, Peter Sellers would have been locked in a movie studio for life, given access to the best talent available, and made to produce Pink Panther comedies through eternity. Once this series hit its stride (forget the first two, *The Pink Panther* and *Shot in the Dark*), the Pink Panther films contained some of the most sublime physical business and verbal silliness of the past forty years.

The best of the lot were *Return of the Pink Panther* (1975) and *The Pink Panther Strikes Again* (1976), numbers three and four in the series. Alas, this was almost the end, as Sellers died long before his time, in 1980. Plots hardly matter in these movies, as both films feature Sellers's Inspector Clouseau bumbling and fumbling his way to the brilliant resolution of another international crime mystery. The Panther movies' appeal lies in the charming goofiness of Sellers's character and the fact that he creates a delightfully ingratiating buffoon in which we can clearly see ourselves.

A very modern comedy of manners and mores, *Tootsie* (1982), features a struggling actor (Dustin Hoffman) forced to pass as a woman to land a lead role in a popular, long-running television soap opera. The Dorothy Michaels' character that Hoffman creates is a terrific comic invention – a strong, winning personality who stands apart from easy male-as-female conventions, giving the plot a sharp, satirical edge to go along with its broad physical comedy.

Modern Masters Allen and Simon

When it comes to sharing the films of modern comic master Woody Allen with children, parents are stuck with some difficult choices between movies that are clever but culturally remote (*Purple Rose of Cairo*) and those dappled with sexual allusions that are dicey for even the most progressive households (*Annie Hall*).

An excellent solution is *Bananas* (1971), made when Allen was still perfecting his filmmaking skills and relying on his sour-jester stand-up persona to provide his movies' substance.

Allen plays Fielding Melish, a bored corporate bureaucrat who falls for a left-wing activist (Louise Lasser), quits his job, goes off to join a Latin American revolution, and becomes the country's president when the revolution succeeds. *Bananas* includes an inspired bit of Allen looniness in which, serving as his own trial lawyer, he interrogates himself and then is forced to be gagged while he questions a hostile witness – managing to reduce the witness to tears with his relentless (if inaudible) questioning.

(Another broadly accessible Allen comedy, *Broadway Danny Rose,* is discussed in our section on backstage dramas.)

The most prolific source of film comedy over the past twenty years has been Neil Simon, a writer who, like Allen and Brooks, got his start as a contributor to the Sid Caesar-Imogene Coca "Your Show of Shows" television series in the 1950s. Simon's breakthrough hit was *The Odd Couple,* a work probably most familiar as a long-running TV series.

Originally, *The Odd Couple* was an enormously popular Broadway play, a work that gave theatrical comedy a smart aleck, streetwise jolt and contributed its own small part to the cosmic cultural revolution of the 1960s (it opened in 1964). The theatrical *Odd Couple* was faithfully captured in a 1968 film version starring Jack Lemmon and Walter Matthau as Felix Unger and Oscar Madison, the mismatched divorced roommates for whom life is a perpetual mid-life crisis. (Matthau had starred in the original play, with Art Carney as Felix.) The film shows author Simon doing what he does best – creating believable human situations that allow him room to hurtle characters at each other like psychotic bumper cars and pepper the landscape with one-liners that career like shrapnel in an interpersonal combat zone.

(Career note: Walter Matthau is an underappreciated, workhorse performer who has contributed his grumpy cynicism to a number of classy productions. Successful as both a leading man and second banana, he has added his avuncular presence to many fine films and can always be guaranteed to provide a memorable chuckle or two. While best known for comedies, Matthau has appeared in films dealing with politics (*Fail-Safe* and *First Monday in October*), backstage show biz (*A Face in the Crowd*), and Western mythology (*Lonely Are the Brave*). For other Matthau films of interest for family viewing, see Appendix B.)

Simon's best film comedy is *The Goodbye Girl* (1977), which dwells on a situation similar to the unseemly roommate setup of *The Odd Couple.* An aspiring Chicago actor (Richard Dreyfuss) shows up in New York, only to find the apartment he has sublet occupied by the departed renter's jilted lover (Marsha Mason) and her young daughter (Quinn Cummings). Written for the screen as a vehicle for Mason, Simon's wife at the time, *The Goodbye Girl* blends a brisk comedy on social relationships and the theater with a sweetly affecting romance. The talented Cummings contributes a feisty child's point of view to the proceedings and will be a hit with young viewers.

Finally and fittingly, a leading candidate for the flat-out funniest film of the past twenty-five years is *My Favorite Year* (1982), which takes us back to the early days of live network television, when everything was fresh and largely spontaneous. The movie's setting is a weekly comedy-variety show modeled after the "Your Show of Shows" series that nurtured Simon, Brooks, and Allen. Its plot concerns an appearance on the show by a legendary but fading movie star (Peter O'Toole) and the crazy adventures of a young writer (Mark Linn-Baker) assigned to make sure the actor stays on his good behavior. O'Toole plays the aging, drunkard star to perfection, and the whole piece rocks with the kind of inspired silliness and broad slapstick too seldom seen nowadays.

Rebellious Youth

In these days when every other film released seems to concern young people in some state of personal rebellion, parents and children will enjoy watching how youth cultures were depicted in previous decades — including the 1950s and 1960s, when many of today's parents came of age. These earlier "rebellious youth" films differ most from modern variants in that they were made for an older audience and look at their young subjects with distance and perspective.

Here we find the "rebellions" are given some sensible purpose and context, lifting them above the posturing found in many modern youth movies. Kids, today, can't help but be impressed by the fact that protests, grievances, and contentious attitudes are not original with their generation and that they are not the first to challenge established authority.

Good Kids Gone Wrong

Rebellious, urban youth, 1930s style, is best depicted in *Angels with Dirty Faces* (1938), featuring James Cagney as Rocky Sullivan, a bad kid who grows up to be worse. After a wayward youth in which he does time for train robbery and other minor offenses, Rocky becomes a rapacious, bootlegging racketeer and is soon idolized by a gang of local youths whom he schools in the basics of criminality.

Also vying for the boys' attention is Father Jerry Connelly (Pat O'Brien), who grew up on the New York streets as Rocky's pal and has maintained a lifelong friendship with him. After securing Rocky's pledge to stop corrupting the kids, Father Jerry implores Rocky – in jail and condemned to die for murder – to show remorse as he goes to the electric chair, so the local street kids won't view him as a role model. Rocky agrees, and the next morning's headlines blare, "Rocky Dies Yellow!"

In *Boys Town* (1936), another Catholic priest in another 1930s melodrama about wayward urban youth, actually utters the words that earmarked most early Hollywood films of this type: "There's no such thing as a bad boy." The priest here is Father Edward Flanagan (Spencer Tracy, in an Oscar-winning role), a real-life cleric who founded a famous home for abandoned boys on the outskirts of Omaha, Nebraska. In the movie, the philosophy behind Boys Town is sorely tested by the arrival of a difficult punk, Whitey Marsh (Mickey Rooney), who decides the Boys Town boys are a bunch of saps for falling for Father Flanagan's line.

In the next decade, a popular slum-kid-gone-bad melodrama, *Knock on Any Door* (1949), was to feature a young rebel character closer in style to kids of the 1960s than to those of the 1930s. Whereas '30s kids like Rocky Sullivan and Whitey Marsh, for all their tough criminality, are seen as essentially good-hearted, there is no such comfort in the portrait of Nick Romano (John Derek). Romano's self-centered rebellion is driven consciously by economic forces and by his sense that these forces, harnessed to his personal charisma, can help him manipulate the straight world for substantial personal gain. Twenty years later, he might well have been a rock promoter, condo developer, or drug kingpin.

In the film, Romano talks his well-intentioned attorney (Humphrey Bogart) into believing that he isn't guilty of killing a policeman, but later confesses under cross-examination on the stand that he did shoot the officer. While the film's theme is that slum conditions breed criminals like Romano (that is, one can be found behind "any door"), the point also comes through that youthful rebellion, whether criminal or not, is a matter of personal style, as exemplified by Romano's famous motto "Live fast, die young, and have a good-looking corpse."

In the 1950s, Hollywood began realizing that contemporary young rebels were products of a rapidly growing, national youth culture and could be packaged to become cultural heroes. The first picture to effectively exploit this reality was *The Wild One* (1954) in which an outlaw biker gang terrorizes a small California town. This movie gave mainstream America its first taste of the Hells Angels-type gangs that would roar down the nation's interstates in the 1960s.

Led by sullen, misunderstood rebel Johnny Staebler (Marlon Brando), the Black Rebels Motorcycle Club members are remarkably tame in comparison to what was actually to come. But the Rebels are unmistakably an extended family, a gang of like-minded, working-class, young men and women who, when the weekend comes, "have to just go, no one place, just lay something down." Like Nick Romano, their rebellion is as much a matter of style as content, as the bikers mostly want to be left alone to pursue a lifestyle that is decidedly out of the mainstream.

While *The Wild One* was alarming the nation with the threat of marauding outlaw bikers, *The Blackboard Jungle* (1955) was soon to scare audiences over what was going on with young street kids in our big cities. No longer misguided, dirty-faced angels, these were tough punks who assaulted female teachers in the library, beat up male teachers in dark alleys, and got hopped up on cheap wine before coming to class. And proving that filmmakers knew that their characters were plugged into a culture that was big and going to get bigger, *The Blackboard Jungle*'s sound track had something new playing behind the opening titles — Bill Haley's "Rock Around the Clock," the nation's first monster rock hit.

Set at an all-boys vocational school in New York City, *The Blackboard Jungle* relates the first few weeks in a new school year and the experiences of rookie teacher Richard Dadier (Glenn Ford). Dadier is a tough World War II vet and not about to give in to the classroom rebels. By movie's end, he has the riffraff expelled and the rest of them discussing "Jack and the Beanstalk" and performing in the Christmas pageant. This may be typical Hollywood sugarcoating, but there is a nasty edge to the rebel characters that gives us a fleeting glimpse of things to come. And in Sidney Poitier's cynical ghetto kid Greg Miller, we see the first stirrings of African American consciousness.

For most kids growing up in the 1950s, there was only one true screen rebel: the moody, volatile antihero that James Dean created in the bristly epic *Rebel without a Cause* (1955). *Rebel* was the first film to show that not all troubled kids rode Harleys or beat up teachers and that they came from the well-manicured suburbs as well as unruly city slums. In fact, what was so troubling about Dean's rebel was that his life was so overwhelmingly normal and characteristic of everything that responsible, well-meaning parents desired for their children.

But Dean's Jim wanted some substance to life that connected with the real world and not the hermetically sealed suburban existence that his parents, and millions of others, so coveted. Dean's anger and anguish were humanly real, a virtual catalog of teenage angst and not at all like the whimsical rebel/prankster poses of today's Ferris Bueller types. It was a disturbing portrait and a luminous warning signal to American parents, who were to see a whole generation of rebellious Jims vanish into the counterculture a decade later.

(Career note: James Dean's other two starring roles were variations on his *Rebel without a Cause* character. In *East of Eden* (1955), Dean plays an emotionally misfit boy who is desperate for his father's love and driven to understand his mother's fall from the family Eden. In *Giant* (1956), Dean appears as a poor oil wildcatter whose sudden good fortune transforms the story's balance of power and alters the destinies of the principal players. This was Dean's most versatile role, allowing him to capture the rude charm of a raw-boned Texan and age convincingly by more than thirty years.)

Musical Rebels

Rebellious youth has never been depicted in a more unseemly setting than in 1961's *West Side Story,* deservingly respected as one of the great musicals of stage and screen. The subjects are similar to those of *The Blackboard Jungle:* New York street youths, the products of first generation immigrant families, unwanted by established white society, and forced back on their own ethnic and generational tribes for cultural sustenance.

What makes their depiction in *West Side Story* work so brilliantly is that the musical's creators tap into that pounding flow of energy, fed by the hormonal thaws of spring, that characterizes young people everywhere. Here it happens to be the Upper West Side of Manhattan in the 1950s and concerns rival gangs of Puerto Rican and Italian kids and the Romeo and Juliet-style love affair that springs up between two of their members (Richard Beymer and Natalie Wood).

Warring gang members are not commonly found singing and dancing their way through city streets, but the magic of *West Side Story* is that viewers are quickly elevated to the production's special level of reality, where singing and dancing are the only imaginable extensions of the young rebels' visceral emotional energy. *West Side Story* should be high up on any family's list of must-see movies, and only gets better with each re-viewing.

Monsters and Aliens

Allowing a filmmaker to make a movie about monsters is like giving a kid the best new toy in the world for Christmas. Both react with glee, gratitude, and inventive play, and exude sheer joy at having absolute control of something wonderful and unexpected. And the results can be just as much fun for the whole family to watch.

Filmmakers began seizing these opportunities as soon as movies had sound, with three of the greatest monster movies of all time (*Frankenstein, Dracula,* and *King Kong*) produced soon after talkies arrived. They were quality productions back then, and can easily hold their own with today's creature features.

Following the monster classics of the 1930s and early 1940s, however, the genre was dominated by lifeless imitations (*The Brides of Dracula*), campy howlers (*Rodan*), and sci-fi flops in which the monsters were more "fi" than "sci" (*I Was a Teenage Werewolf*). In the 1970s, the genre was rescued from its B-movie fate by the advent of computerized special effects and advanced production techniques, along with the realization by ambitious, talented film directors that great monsters can be used to make great movies. Thus, in more recent years, we have had hit films featuring such fascinating creatures as the gargantuan shark in *Jaws* and the huge, tunneling serpents in *Tremors.*

The films we list here provide a selection of recent and not-so-recent films that reflect the best of this time-honored movie genre. Of course, as always, you need to be the judge of your child's ability to enjoy this movie fun without lingering nightmares.

Early Monster Classics

Frankenstein (1931) is most people's idea of the definitive monster movie. It is the story of mad scientist Henry Frankenstein (Colin Clive), who pays grave robbers to steal brains, implants them in corpses, and then taps celestial powers to zap the specimens and create life in his watchtower laboratory. No matter how often filmmakers try to update, remake, and outdo it, the original *Frankenstein* remains the best, enduring because it is a wise and considerate film about how we deal with the unknown and because (as the audience knows) the monster is plainly not the evil force that Dr. Frankenstein's terrified neighbors perceive him to be. In addition, the monster is invested with an endearing soul and spirit by actor Boris Karloff, in a vibrant nonspeaking performance.

The first *Frankenstein* was followed by a sequel, *The Bride of Frankenstein* (1935), a deft and accomplished film in which the monster learns to speak (Karloff offers a stunning encore performance) and goes galumphing through the English countryside, where he encounters a blind hermit, a small girl, and others who help us to see the creature through unbiased eyes. Also, of course, the monster is given a mate (Elsa Lanchester), leading to one of the most unusual and touching romantic relationships on film.

The other *Frankenstein* spinoff that should be noted is 1974's *Young Frankenstein*, a funny, loving parody in which writer-director Mel Brooks manages to update the basic story and give it a satirical spin that does nothing to diminish the original. For more on this sequel, see the section on great comedy films.

The original *Dracula* (1931) is memorable for another fine performance and for its spectral, wispy atmospherics. First we encounter Bela Lugosi's wicked count on a grand staircase in his Transylvanian castle, greeting a visitor by intoning for the ages, "I am . . . Dracula." Like *Frankenstein, Dracula* is barely over an hour long and is chock-full of helpful tidbits of vampire lore. (First of all, they don't like to be called vampires, but rather "the undead.")

Third in the triumvirate of epic man/monster creations is Lon Chaney, Jr.'s lead character in *The Wolf Man* (1941). Chaney plays a perfectly normal, likable guy who is bitten by a werewolf (Lugosi) one night on the moors and, much against his wishes, turns into a werewolf himself. *The Wolf Man*'s focus is more on the human drama of the situation than on baroque scare tactics, as Chaney attempts to cope with his bizarre new condition without losing his fiancee (Evelyn Ankers) or upsetting his doting father (Claude Rains).

From Human to Nonhuman

In the realm of nonhuman monsters, the enormous ape in *King Kong* (1933) – "The Eighth Wonder of the World" – remains the definitive colossus. He is a touchingly sensitive brute whose cinematic deeds, even measured against today's sophisticated special effects, remain breathtaking. Among them are the battle with Tyrannosaurus rex, breaking loose in a Broadway theater, and, of course, Kong's duel with the biplanes while standing atop the Empire State Building.

King Kong is a triumph in creative, resourceful filmmaking that conveys a message that is strikingly appropriate for today's environmentally conscious culture. Clearly, viewers are meant to sympathize with Kong's predicament and recoil at his shameless exploitation, as he is plucked from his native habitat in the East Indies and brought back to New York City for the pleasure of gawking multitudes and the enrichment of movie producer Carl Denham (Robert Armstrong).

A 1950s effort to recapture the Kong charisma, *Godzilla* (1956) is at least as interesting for the way it was produced as for the special effects that merit its viewing. The original Japanese production, released in 1954, was acquired by American distributors who grafted on new footage featuring American actor Raymond Burr and unwittingly created a minor cult classic, on its re-release in the United States.

The title monster is a four-hundred-foot lizard that has been slumbering at the bottom of the Pacific since the Jurassic period, only to be awakened by the constant boom-boom-boom of H-bomb testing. Angry at being disturbed, Godzilla lashes out at the nearest thing at hand, which happens to be downtown Tokyo. Unlike *King Kong* and the other films listed here, *Godzilla* is primitive filmmaking, its chief salvation being ambitious special effects and sheer outrageousness.

In the modern era, *Jaws* (1975) is renowned as the film that made director Steven Spielberg a success and made monster movies broadly respectable again. From the opening beach-party midnight swim through the last man-against-monster showdown, the film is a triumph of goose-pimpling terror. Unlike the producers of *King Kong,* who were intent on humanizing their beast, Spielberg keeps his monster as mysterious as possible and feeds the suspense by having the white shark remain largely unseen until the movie's last few minutes.

What keeps *Jaws* from being just another modern, mechanical creep show is Spielberg's story-telling skill, with its subplot of greedy townspeople not wanting to risk losing tourist dollars. The movie is highlighted by the slick performances of Roy Scheider as the dedicated local cop, Richard Dreyfuss as the earnest ichthyologist, and Robert Shaw as the salty shark fighter.

A monster movie that comes close to matching *Jaws* for both chilly thrills and delicious story telling is the 1990 sleeper *Tremors.* Set in the Southwest desert, *Tremors* features a family of gargantuan burrowing reptiles that terrorize a small, isolated town that bears the grimly ironic name, Perfection.

In addition to its for-real chills, *Tremors* is executed with goofy good humor, most of it involving the two thick-headed drifters who first encounter the underground monsters (Kevin Bacon and Fred Ward) and including an uproarious debate as to the beasts' likely origins and the most fitting names for them. Like the shark in *Jaws,* the creatures in *Tremors* remain largely unseen and are all the more terrifying for it.

Alien Creatures Through The Years

Movies featuring alien creatures are of special interest in their demonstration of how, historically, cultures have been defined in part by their treatment of outsiders. Collective American attitudes toward outsiders at any given moment have long been reflected in motion pictures that present outsiders in the most abstract sense possible – as beings from another world.

Extraterrestrials are ideal stand-ins for all of society's social biases. Whether depicted as slithering blobs or hydra-headed monsters, Hollywood-style extraterrestrials always symbolize a mysterious presence that threatens the social status quo and echo popular social attitudes toward real-world "outsider" groups. From the malevolent paranoia of post-World War II to the blissed-out wonderment of the 1960s, Hollywood movies about alien forces present a chronicle of the widely-shared biases of the past forty years.

For example, to a nation that had just witnessed Dunkirk, Pearl Harbor, D-Day, and Hiroshima, an aggressive invading alien force meant only one thing – war! What could be worse than a war in which our weapons were useless, our troops helpless, and the alien force seemingly invincible.

This is the basic plot structure of *War of the Worlds* (1953), a vividly updated version of H. G. Wells's classic novel. The movie begins with narrator Sir Cedric Hardwicke talking about "the terrible weapons of superscience" and how they would soon be needed to fight an invasion from Mars, the mysterious red planet that was "in the last stages of exhaustion," its inhabitants "searching for another world to migrate to."

Next we see a menacing craft landing near a small California town, its occupants soon vaporizing the townspeople. Before long, spacecraft are landing all over the world, wiping out huge cities, pulverizing vast populations, defeating mighty armies. This was scary stuff for a nation that had recently fought a world war against dictatorial rule, and the warning implicit in *War of the Worlds* was that America could not let its guard down for a minute.

Before long, however, the hot-war mind-set represented by *War of the Worlds* was replaced by a paranoid realization, born of a Cold War fear of communism, that subversive alien forces could silently invade and conquer America without resorting to overt force. As translated on screen in *The Blob* (1958), for example, the scourge was a gelatinous mass that looked innocent enough until it began silently gobbling up everyone who touched it. The movie is great, goopy fun, and notable as the screen debut of Steve McQueen.

Another great movie packed with alien excitement is *Invasion of the Body Snatchers,* first produced at the height of the Cold War (1956) and remade twenty years later with a countercultural twist (1978). In both versions, unseen alien forces plant seeds in fertile U.S. earth, and from these seeds sprout huge pods bearing anatomically correct physical duplicates of human beings.

Alien agents surreptitiously place the pods in private homes to absorb the human inhabitants' minds while they are sleeping. The vanquished earthlings are then "reborn" into this world without human emotions, thoughts, or feelings. The aliens' objective is to create a world where everyone thinks and acts exactly the same and personal independence is unknown. Then the alien masters will show themselves and complete their conquest.

Both versions of *Body Snatchers* are unique among alien movies in that the menace being perpetrated is intellectual and not physical, with earthlings in no apparent bodily danger until their minds are quietly absorbed and they are put away for a long rest. Just what this insidious, invisible force was supposed to represent as a cultural metaphor varied in the two movies. In the 1956 version, the aliens represent the forces of socialist regimentation, and in the 1978 film, they represent cultural conformism.

Changing Attitudes Toward Aliens

Revisionist aliens-as-good-guys attitudes were in evidence in Hollywood as far back as 1951's *The Day the Earth Stood Still.* Here, a gracious, courtly alien named Klaatu (Michael Rennie) lands his spaceship on the Mall in Washington, D.C., and tries to warn humankind about the irresponsible use of atomic energy. Some believe Klaatu, rallying to his cause; others are suspicious and shoot him. (For more on this movie, see our discussion of movies dealing with science gone amok.)

The good alien idea was brought spectacularly into the mainstream years later by Steven Spielberg in two of the most popular films ever made: *Close Encounters of the Third Kind* (1977) and *E.T.— The Extra-Terrestrial* (1982). Although produced long after the flowering of the mid-1960s cultural revolution, these movies reflect attitudes central to that decade. Both the childlike Roy (Richard Dreyfuss) in *Close Encounters* and the remarkably mature child Elliott (Henry Thomas) in *E.T.* are positive-minded individuals. They are predisposed to believe the best of others (whether earthlings or aliens) and willing to defy higher authorities, including the federal government, in affirming their beliefs.

Close Encounters is a revisionist film in several regards, including its treatment of unidentified flying objects (UFOs) as serious phenomena and not as off-the-wall fantasies of the lunatic fringe. Based on an investigative book by leading UFO authority, J. Allen Hynek, director Spielberg uses his film to elevate flying-saucer buffs to prophet status and places them in the vanguard of those trying to make peaceful contact with other worlds. When contact comes, Spielberg speculates, it will not be by means of radio signals, binary code, or algorithms; it will be through an intergalactic language based on tonal music. Brilliant!

While more of a transgenerational fable than the more serious-minded *Close Encounters, E.T.* is an extension of Spielberg's earlier film in terms of driving home the point that unusual space creatures are not to be feared and fought but may be among us for the most benign reasons, such as looking for a way to get home. There is no stronger cinematic statement for tolerance, acceptance, and understanding than that found in *E.T.,* and the fact that it is imparted without resorting to heavy-handed preaching only adds to the movie's great charm.

Race Relations

Given that social issue movies are considered bad box office draws, it is surprising that several quality films dealing with black-white relations have been made at all. You will look in vain for their like among major films dealing with poverty, homelessness, unemployment, and government abuse of individual rights. The Hollywood record is not unblemished on the racial matter, however. Without the acting career of Sidney Poitier and the go-to-hell leadership of producer/director Stanley Kramer, there would be far less to write about.

Before the 1960s, there was virtually nothing to write about. Blacks were either shamefully pigeonholed as slaves, servants, or minstrels in mainstream movies or shuffled off to all-black features marketed to all-black audiences — Hollywood's equivalent of baseball's Negro Leagues. Rarely were black performers accorded screen parity with their white counterparts by being cast in roles where race was irrelevant (Dooley Wilson's piano player in *Casablanca* being a notable example of a part that could have been cast in any color).

Even in postwar Hollywood, where liberal humanism was pervasive and powerful, race relations received little coverage. A laudable exception was *Home of the Brave* (1949), a frank, dramatic Stanley Kramer production that exposes American racial prejudice through the microcosm of a five-man U.S. Army unit sent on a secret mission in the South Pacific during World War II. One of the GIs is a black soldier (James Edwards); his four white buddies demonstrate a range of social attitudes — from so-what acceptance to outright bigotry — in their reactions to this man on whom their lives come to depend.

Pioneering Poitier

Sidney Poitier came to Hollywood in 1950 to debut in the gangster picture *No Way Out* and then alternated between film, stage, and television work before establishing his screenstar presence as a sensitive delinquent in 1955's *The Blackboard Jungle* (see the discussion of movies about rebellious youth). Poitier has been a motion picture fixture ever since, a subtle, stylish performer whose gracious presence has ennobled several second-rate projects and enhanced a number of top-drawer efforts.

The first feature in Poitier's exemplary career to overtly deal with racial attitudes was *The Defiant Ones* (1958), another effort by producer/director Kramer to slap movie audiences awake on the subject of black-white relations. In this chase melodrama, Poitier and Tony Curtis escape from a prison road gang and scramble to freedom, bound by a length of chain and a dependence on each other that becomes more emotional than logistical as their flight progresses.

Time has improved *The Defiant Ones,* allowing the explosive racial message to recede in importance in favor of the rich supporting-player characterizations and the knuckle-gnawing suspense. Even so, Curtis's sharp retort to the unshackled Poitier — "there's still a chain" — cuts to the core of racial tolerance as cleanly now as it did thirty-plus years ago.

Lillies of the Field (1963) offers a double-edged racial message, with Poitier playing an itinerant handyman who is taken in by an order of immigrant German nuns in a Hispanic village in the Southwest and helps earn his keep by building them a chapel. While the skeptical local whites are compelled to accept Poitier as a job boss in their midst, he in turn is sensitized to the differing ways of the ascetic nuns and the native Hispanics.

A film of refreshing simplicity, *Lillies of the Field* is the kind of "little picture" that Hollywood has not been able to afford to produce in recent years. Both protagonists and antagonists are treated with sensitivity and respect, and the moral messages regarding interpersonal relations and community bonding are earnestly unadorned. For all that, *Lillies* was a huge hit for its time, winning Poitier his one best actor Oscar and capturing nominations as best picture and best supporting actress (for Lilia Skala, as the mother superior).

Another exemplary picture of this period is the 1962 feature *To Kill a Mockingbird,* a warm and lovely film that shows compassion in depicting the fabric of personal emotions that informed racial attitudes in the pre-1960s rural South. Beneath its overlay of courtroom melodrama, *To Kill a Mockingbird* is a vividly dramatic homily about accepting individuals for themselves and ignoring the stereotypes, rumors, and suspicions that others may project on them. The people "teaching" this lesson are widowed attorney Atticus Finch (Gregory Peck) and his two children, Scout and Jim (Mary Badham and Philip Alford). The two individuals whom they embrace and encourage others to accept are a black man (Brock Peters) falsely accused of rape and a white mentally-challenged man (Robert Duvall, in his screen debut) falsely rumored to be terrorizing the town at night.

Based on Harper Lee's Pulitzer prize-winning novel, *To Kill a Mockingbird* is a gentle film of great moral urgency. If Hollywood had to hold up one film from among the thousands it has produced that best exemplifies the dramatic embodiment of noble and decent human values, this could well be it.

(One racial curio of this period is the 1964 film version of John Howard Griffin's first-person book *Black Like Me.* In this film, the explosive issue of prejudice is addressed through the eyes of a white newspaper reporter who chemically alters his skin pigment to experience and write about his treatment as a "black" in the South. While it seems hopelessly trivial in light of subsequent events, both book and movie were high-impact media fare for their time.)

Reflecting 1960s Turmoil

Racial turmoil was rapidly cresting in the mid-1960s, as civil rights demonstrations proliferated, rhetoric became heated, and urban riots were commonplace. Hollywood has thus far resisted using the events of this period as historical subject matter, with the exception of *Mississippi Burning* (1988), which begins as a film about the 1963 disappearance of three northern civil rights workers near Philadelphia, Mississippi, and disintegrates into a disappointing (and strongly R-rated) good-cop/bad-cop buddy film.

The year 1967 became a watershed for major motion pictures dealing with racial themes — as well as for actor Poitier. He was the key player in two cele-brated films that approached black-white relations from directions that were polar opposites.

Winner of the 1967 best picture Oscar, *In the Heat of the Night* is a murder mystery set in an all-purpose southern town, with stranger Poitier an instant suspect in the shooting death of a local white man. It turns out that Poitier is a Pennsylvania policeman passing through town on business, and, after over-coming the initial distrust, he stays around for a few days to help the local sheriff (Rod Steiger) break the case. (Poitier followed up with two sequels to the Oscar-winning picture — *They Call Me Mister Tibbs!* and *The Organization* — while the original movie later leant itself to a popular 1980s TV series of the same name.)

As with the majority of other films on this list, *In the Heat of the Night* is set in the Deep South and peopled with nasty, deep-fried southerners. Indeed, it is an irony of progressive filmmaking that the character of the fat, drawling southern redneck — usually called Bubba and found driving a pickup truck with a gun rack — has become as pernicious and unthinking a stereotype as any the movies have invented.

The year 1967 also produced a film that shook blame-the-South attitudes to their cozy core, the celebrated *Guess Who's Coming to Dinner.* Poitier again is the star, and Stanley Kramer the producer/director. *Dinner* removes black-white conflict from the easy confines of the small-town South and thrusts it boldly into the tony drawing rooms of filthy-rich San Francisco, with Poitier engaged to marry the squeaky-clean daughter of smugly, progressive parents Spencer Tracy and Katharine Hepburn.

Both *In the Heat of the Night* and *Guess Who's Coming to Dinner* stand the test of time, but the latter's endurance is more impressive. Derided by some as a mawkish cartoon at its release in the hypersensitive 1960s, the film emerges twenty-plus years later as a caring, thoughtful effort to translate universal con-cerns into intensely personal struggles. And while Tracy and Hepburn won acclaim for their last performance together, it is Poitier's integrity as a performer that ties the picture together and makes it whole.

Legal Underpinnings of Struggle

Poitier's most recent contribution to movies about race relations is his role as NAACP chief legal counsel Thurgood Marshall in the outstanding made-for-TV drama *Separate But Equal* (1991). This lengthy (193 minutes), detailed, meticulously evenhanded account of a landmark school desegregation case of the early 1950s is also one-of-a-kind cinema. It dramatizes the contributions made to the civil rights cause by the poor black sharecroppers who initiated the Clarendon County, South Carolina, case, as well as the NAACP's wealthy white liberal benefactors who allowed Marshall and his legal team to carry the battle to the U.S. Supreme Court. *Separate But Equal* differs from such highly dramatic fare as *Mississippi Burning* and *In the Heat of the Night* in responsibly and fairly detailing the deep-rooted social biases that underlie antiblack prejudice and the painstaking legal campaign that tried to destroy them.

For all their earnest efforts to advance the cause of interracial harmony, the cruel reality is that all of these films were overwhelmingly the work of white producers, writers, and directors. Until very recently, Hollywood was a lily-white establishment that, whatever the residents' avowed politics, was essentially closed to blacks. This has changed over the past half-dozen years, and the change will be accelerated as more talented black directors and writers come on the scene and their films find large bi-racial audiences.

Real-Life Heroes

Movies are able to present us with a spectacular, idealized vision of ourselves, an opportunity to project our fantasy-fed self-images onto the larger-than-life images dancing before us on the silver screen. This is especially true in the movies' presentation of real-life heroes. Not content that these men and women performed heroic deeds, Hollywood must embroider the legends, creating mythic portraits that tell as much about the audience as the subject. Following a popular war, we have *To Hell and Back;* following an unpopular war, we have *Born on the Fourth of July.*

The challenge that scriptwriters and directors face in capturing real-life heroes on-screen is to identify some personal qualities that transform mere mortals into living legends and then depict those qualities in a credible, entertaining story. The following movies present a believable (if exaggerated) depiction of "ordinary" men and women who performed extraordinary acts.

Heroes in Revolutionary Situations

An ideal place to begin is *Lawrence of Arabia* (1962), recently reissued on video with enhanced color, added footage, and a "letter-box" format that preserves the dimensions of the wide-screen original (but sacrifices the intimacy of close-up scenes).

Lawrence (spectacularly played by Peter O'Toole) was a low-ranking British officer based in Cairo who, during World War I, single-handedly molded feuding Arab tribes into a fighting force that drove the pro-German Turks from the Middle East. Lawrence's experience is the realization of every dilettante's fantasy: the chance to use obscure knowledge and bookish perspective in the field among living, breathing subjects. Lawrence's greatness is rooted in his personal vision of a mighty pan-Arabic nation and fed by unyielding messianic determination.

Lawrence's obsession is expressed in the film by King Faisal (Alec Guinness) as a "fascination with desolate places," a particularly British trait that has been irresistible to filmmakers. It is to be found in such real-life film subjects as military leader Charles George "Chinese" Gordon (Charlton Heston) in *Khartoum* (1966), missionary David Livingstone (Cedric Hardwicke) in *Stanley and Livingstone* (1939), and explorer Richard Burton (Patrick Bergin) in *Mountains of the Moon* (1990).

Stanley Kubrick's *Spartacus* (1960) tells the story of a first-century B.C. gladiator who assumed leadership of a spontaneous uprising of Roman slaves seeking to return to their native lands. Kirk Douglas's Spartacus is no sophisticated political visionary like T. E. Lawrence but an accidental leader whose heroic simplicity and singularity of purpose are counterposed against the duplicity, corruption, and intrigue of the leaders of republican Rome.

Another revolutionary hero artfully captured on film is Emiliano Zapata, the uneducated field hand who led a bloody peasant revolt against Mexico's governing dictatorship in the early 1900s. His story is told in *Viva Zapata!* (1952), and he is played by Marlon Brando, in an astonishing early-career performance. This Zapata may, like Spartacus, be an accidental leader, but he grows quickly to become a savvy political strategist military tactician. He is a peasant forced by circumstance to help shape historic events, and who would probably otherwise have remained in the fields. *Viva Zapata!* is a depiction of the dynamics of popular revolution as seen through the eyes of conventional Hollywood liberalism and is especially adept at showing the internal battles that can undermine a rebellion and frustrate its leaders.

Another Brando film that focuses on revolution in Latin America is the 1969 feature *Burn!*, directed and coauthored by the Italian filmmaker Gillo Pontecorvo. *Burn!* is set in a fictional Caribbean nation 150 years ago and concerns the real-life exploits of a British adventurer named William Walker as he helps his employer, a British sugar combine, foment a doomed-to-fail revolution that will create a political and economic climate more to the company's liking.

A revolutionary hero of a markedly different stripe is portrayed in Richard Attenborough's meticulous epic *Gandhi* (1982). One of the few films to treat modern Third World leaders in an intelligent, sympathetic light, this 188-minute movie follows the shy, ascetic Mohandas Gandhi from his days as a young lawyer defending minority Indians in South Africa to his success in leading India out of the British Commonwealth and into full independence following World War II.

Movies being movies, we do not often see a film portraying a heroic leader whose whole philosophy is founded on nonviolence, making *Gandhi,* and its Oscar-winning reception, all the more commendable. Not only does it depict the roots, shape, and dramatic majesty of Gandhi's pacifist activism, but it also manages to make his story cinematically compelling and interesting.

Heroes From American History

The great success of *The Spirit of St. Louis* (1957) and its star James Stewart is in conveying the significance of Charles A. Lindbergh's transatlantic flight in 1927 and in evoking the personal qualities that induced the young pilot to raise the money, build the plane, and make the four-thousand-mile flight alone and without instruments (or even windows). Lindbergh was the most celebrated international figure of his day, a symbol of a postwar industrial America for which all things were possible, and his flight caught the fancy of a world ready to forge intimate global links of travel, commerce, and communication.

In the realm of military heroics, movies have tended to treat real-life heroes in the context of major battles and not as subjects of film biographies. The most successful exception is *Patton* (1970), a film of extraordinary artistic achievement whose individual scenes stand alone as vivid set pieces and collectively create a convincing portrait of a unique military hero.

General George S. Patton (George C. Scott) is painted as a classic warrior, a man educated in history and philosophy who saw battle as an ultimate physical challenge between disciplined armies and fought according to rules grounded in medieval chivalry and personal honor. He is a man at ease with command and the black and white reality of battle, but ill-equipped to deal with a multinational military bureaucracy governed by sophisticated geopolitical concerns.

(Career note: Patton is the pinnacle of movie achievement for Scott, a highly respected stage actor whose limited film work is otherwise spotty. Fittingly, he won an Oscar for *Patton,* and characteristically, he refused the award, saying that acting is a sufficiently rugged career without actors having to be placed in artificial competition with each other. Other Scott films discussed in this book include *Anatomy of a Murder,* in the courtroom drama section, and *Dr. Strangelove,* discussed with other films having political themes.)

For a different brand of military heroism, compare *MacArthur* (1977), the film biography of another World War II hero, General Douglas MacArthur (Gregory Peck). This American general is an overtly political animal, embracing a social and economic philosophy that he is not afraid to articulate and practice, including during his stint as postwar governor of Japan. In this film, MacArthur's greatest fights are not against mighty armies, but are battles for devout philosophical principles against perceived ideological enemies (including U.S. President Harry Truman).

Military heroism in the lower ranks is presented in *Sergeant York* (1941) and *To Hell and Back* (1955), films that profile the most decorated infantrymen in, respectively, World Wars I and II. The former concerns Tennessee mountain boy Alvin York and stars Gary Cooper in an Academy Award-winning performance; the latter both profiles and stars Texas farm boy Audie Murphy, whose film career was considerably less stellar than his military tour. While the films are different in period and mode of battle, both bring a distinctly American twist to an ancient warrior legend: the simple rustic who sets aside his plow to fight mighty armies and comes back a hero but otherwise unchanged.

For more recent military-related heroics, the best that Hollywood has done is to extol the original seven U.S. astronauts – all military test pilots – and the events leading up to the first manned American space flights in *The Right Stuff* (1983). The movie effectively captures the astronauts' crusade to break out of the NASA role of robotic fly-boys and then manages to depict the excitement and sense of global awe that followed as the "Mercury Seven" ventured into the uncharted reaches of space.

U.S. political heroes have provided far less material for filmmakers than their military counterparts. One glowing exception is *Abe Lincoln in Illinois* (1940), a masterpiece that uses near-documentary clarity and force in presenting the years leading up to Lincoln's presidential election and departure for Washington. Raymond Massey's portrait of Lincoln is legendary, vividly conveying the intellectual force and oratorical genius that takes Lincoln from a life of failure, false starts, and modest success to the leadership of the nation.

Among the few other president-as-subject movies are Woodrow Wilson portrayed in *Wilson,* Franklin D. Roosevelt portrayed in *Sunrise at Campobello,* Dwight D.

Eisenhower portrayed in *The Longest Day,* and John F. Kennedy portrayed in *PT 109.*

Women As Film Heroes

Another hero gap is found in looking for movies about real-life female heroes. One famous candidate is *Saint Joan* (1957), based on the George Bernard Shaw play and featuring newcomer Jean Seberg as the Orleans farm girl who is moved by heavenly voices to lead the French army against occupying English troops – only to be burned at the stake as a witch by a jealous church hierarchy.

In more recent films, real-life women are found as subjects of two quality films that focus on ordinary citizens momentarily thrust into an exhibition of uncommon bravery: nuclear power plant worker Karen Silkwood (Meryl Streep) in *Silkwood* (1983) and Tennessee housewife-turned-activist Marie Ragghianti (Sissy Spacek) in *Marie* (1985).

These two women are similar not only in their brave battle against male-dominated establishments but also in having to deal with emotional domestic situations as they undergo their battles. Both films are discussed at greater length in the section on rebel-with-a-cause movies.

Physically and Mentally Challenged Characters

The world of physically and mentally challenged people, while hardly a Hollywood staple, has been the subject of a number of films that can be rewarding family viewing experiences. Many of them focus on the tearjerker aspects of the human relationships involved instead of on the broader and more substantial issues of how society deals with such people, and they with it.

In this context, the lead character's so-called handicap is a mere variation on that Hollywood staple: the movie hero or heroine who faces a life-threatening illness. This has been the theme of such memorable box office hits as 1939's *Dark Victory* (brain tumor), 1942's *Pride of the Yankees* (lateral arterial sclerosis), 1955's *Interrupted Melody* (polio), 1970's *Love Story* (cancer), 1986's *Duet for One* (multiple sclerosis), and 1991's *Dying Young* (leukemia).

Otherwise, Hollywood is so monumentally oblivious to the presence of mentally and physically challenged people that we rarely see supporting or incidental characters on crutches or in wheelchairs. Only in recent years, with films such as

My Left Foot and *Mask,* have filmmakers moved boldly to present lead characters who defy traditional movie stereotypes and forthrightly address the problems
of physical and mental challenges.

Following is a discussion of these and other impressive, award-winning movies
that stand out from the pack. They feature compelling lead characters who
happen to be physically or mentally challenged, offer insight into how society
treats these individuals, and depict in legitimate, dramatic terms exactly how they
cope with the special situations they face.

Mentally Challenged Movie Characters

The treatment of mental debility in motion pictures has become more sophisticated as society itself has learned to deal with and accept this human phenomenon.
Hollywood has a shameful past of using mentally challenged individuals as a
comical shorthand characterization of some unsavory subculture (the rooster-
crowing, saddle tramp in *True Grit*) or to connote atmospheric regional mystery
(the banjo-strumming, albino rustic in *Deliverance*).

One of the first successful films to feature a mentally challenged character was
Charly (1968), a commercial hit for which Cliff Robertson won an Oscar for best
actor. So intent was Robertson on bringing this story to the screen that he
purchased the film rights after appearing in a television version ("The Two Worlds
of Charlie Gordon") in the early 1960s and spent several years trying to convince
movie studios to produce the film.

Robertson's Charlie Gordon ("Charly" is how he spells his name) is a mentally
challenged bakery worker taking night courses to improve his spelling, vocabulary,
and other cognitive skills. His self-motivation impresses the school's directors to
invite Charly to be a willing patient in a medical experiment designed to overcome
the debilities of retardation by altering a suspected chemical imbalance in the
brain.

The operation is a huge success, and Charly's mental capacity quickly escalates
to near-genius level. He is fired from his menial custodial job when it becomes
clear he is now smarter than the bakery workers who previously taunted him, and
he acquires a love interest, in the person of a devoted teacher (Claire Bloom) who
eventually asks him to marry her.

Charly has elements of soap opera romance and futuristic fantasy (one popular
video guide categorizes the film as science fiction) that tend to dilute its message
about retardation. But the few moments that do address this plot element are

powerful and unforgettable: the cruel practical jokes of the bakery workers, the restaurant patrons' taunting of a clumsy busboy, and Charly's own bitter questioning of why "people who'd never laugh at a blind or crippled man laugh at a moron."

For a simpler, unadorned version of Charlie Gordon's story, we have the Australian feature *Tim* (1979), based on the first novel by Colleen McCollough (*The Thorn Birds*) and featuring an outstanding, presuperstardom performance by Mel Gibson in the title role. *Tim* has no hint of sci-fi razzle-dazzle, nor is there any unseemly only-in-the-movies transformation of its lead character into a sudden genius. Instead, we have a bare bones melodrama of a cheery mentally challenged man and the people who support him with their unquestioning love.

Tim Melville (Gibson) is a landscape laborer in his late twenties who lives with his elderly parents and develops a friendship with middle-aged spinster Mary Horton (Piper Laurie). As their May-December relationship deepens, Mary learns more about the emotional and physical needs of mentally challenged persons, and *Tim* becomes a forceful, intelligent case for treating these persons with respect, patience, and affection.

For all its superficial star power and calculated box office appeal, *Rain Man* (1988) remains at its core the most polished and compelling screen treatment of a mentally challenged person that Hollywood has yet produced. The point is made that Raymond Babbitt (Dustin Hoffman) is not retarded or crazy but – in the words of an on-screen doctor – suffers "a disability that impairs the sensory input and how it's processed." Raymond's affliction is called autism, an extreme form of self-absorption in which the victim creates a personal fantasy world as an escape from reality. Raymond is extremely gifted in the area of mental calculation and mnemonics, creating the seemingly improbable phenomenon of the idiot or autistic savant.

Rain Man is an extended illustration of this phenomenon at work in the world, woven into the larger plot that has Raymond's brother Charlie (Tom Cruise), an unprincipled hustler disinherited by his father, trying to win custody of Raymond and control of the family fortune. Of all the films dealing with mental disabilities, *Rain Man* provides the best insight into understanding and dealing with mentally challenged persons in our society.

(Note to parents: Regrettably, *Rain Man* also suffers from a trait typical of modern movies – the inclusion of profuse and totally unnecessary harsh profanity. This, along with one equally gratuitous bedroom scene, earned the film an R rating and prevents this otherwise instructive, enlightening, and entertaining picture from being universally acceptable for young audiences. Caution is advised.)

The most common physical challenge depicted in feature films is blindness, and is the central subject of the best movie in this theme section: *The Miracle Worker* (1962). This celebrated film, based on the play by William Gibson, stars Oscar winners Patty Duke (best supporting actress) as the blind, deaf, and mute Helen Keller and Anne Bancroft (best actress) as her governess/teacher, Annie Sullivan.

Helen lost her sight and hearing as the result of a severe fever when she was nineteen months old. In the custom of the day (she was born in 1880), her family then treated her as a perpetual infant, with no higher expectation than that she negotiate life with a minimum of harm to herself and discomfort to others. "Half-sister and half mentally defective," sighs her exasperated step-brother James (Andrew Prine). "She really ought to be put away in some asylum."

Instead, Helen's progressive publisher father (Victor Jory) pursues remedial options all the way to Boston's Perkins School for the Blind and contracts for Annie Sullivan to come to the family's home in Tuscumbia, Alabama, to teach his fourteen-year-old daughter to read, speak, and make sense of the world around her. Annie is the perfect match for the bright and willful Helen, a feisty twenty-one-year-old first-generation Irish American, raised in a state orphanage, and herself a victim of blindness that has been only partially cured through surgery.

The Miracle Worker is the story of the growing, loving relationship between Helen and Annie. Their scenes have a powerful primal intensity, propelled by rage at the seemingly arbitrary curses of fate, as Annie labors to have Helen make the intellectual connection between the words she can sign-spell and the objects she can feel. Especially notable are the fierce battle of wills over dining room etiquette and the climactic breakthrough episode that culminates in Annie's spine-tingling cry of triumph: "She knows!"

On a deeper level, *The Miracle Worker* confronts the central issue of how society deals with physically challenged people and shows how they, given the right combination of familial love and access to learning tools, can grow and become productive citizens. Seven years after the events depicted in this movie, Helen Keller produced her first great nonfiction work, *The Story of My Life,* and went on to become a renowned author, lecturer, and advocate for the world's blind population.

An example of how Hollywood has cleverly used blindness as a plot device in a pure-entertainment film is *Wait Until Dark* (1967), which features Audrey Hepburn as a Manhattan housewife who is blinded in a fiery car crash. A year after the accident, Hepburn's photographer husband (Efrem Zimbalist, Jr.) inadvertently comes into possession of a heroin cache, and a trio of bad guys (led by Alan Arkin) invades their home and tries to terrorize Hepburn into handing over the drugs.

The clever plot twist of *Wait Until Dark* is the way in which Hepburn turns her supposed handicap into an advantage in dealing with the thugs. The film may not be about sightlessness as such, but it makes a strong statement that society can best aid blind people by treating them with understanding and consideration, and not with pity.

(Career note: Audrey Hepburn has had only a handful of starring roles since her sensational Oscar-winning debut in 1953's *Roman Holiday,* and none since 1981. *Wait Until Dark* is one of her most enjoyable and entertaining films. Another mentioned in "For Starters" is *Robin and Marian.* See Appendix B for other Hepburn films of interest for family viewing.)

Deafness is another familiar cinematic debility, and three highly honored and widely celebrated films that feature lead characters who cannot hear (or truly speak) are *Johnny Belinda* (1948), *The Heart is a Lonely Hunter* (1968), and *Children of a Lesser God* (1986).

Set in a tiny fishing village on Cape Breton Island, off Nova Scotia, *Johnny Belinda* is as much about the provincial inhabitants' fear of outsiders as it is about the challenges facing its principal character, Belinda MacDonald (Jane Wyman). One of the great tearjerkers from 1940s Hollywood, *Johnny Belinda* tells the moving story of how the Cape Breton farmer's daughter is taught signing and lip-reading by a kindly newly-arrived doctor (Lew Ayres), wins the love and respect of her gruff father (Charles Bickford), and defies the churlish townspeople who want to take away the baby named Johnny Belinda who is born to her as a result of a sadistic rape by a drunken townie (Stephen McNally).

The Heart Is a Lonely Hunter is classic Carson McCullers fiction, set in the small-town South and featuring a precocious young woman (Sondra Locke, in her impressive movie debut) whose intellectual and spiritual growth are hindered by the emotional impoverishment of the community. The central force of McCullers's multilayered plot is John Singer (Alan Arkin), a deaf-mute whose simple goodness allows him to penetrate the lives of his fellows and help them confront their inner demons. Despite its downbeat ending, Hunter excels at demonstrating how a seemingly handicapped individual can nurture other personal qualities that make him a valuable and treasured member of the community.

Of the three films in this sequence, *Children of a Lesser God* is the one whose plot deals most directly with deafness and deaf individuals. The central figures are speech teacher James Leeds (William Hurt) and Sarah Norman (Marlee Matlin), a beautiful, mysterious deaf woman who graduated from the school where James comes to teach and now works there as a custodian. As their physical relationship develops, Leeds pushes Sarah to stop relying totally on signing for communication and to learn to speak — something she refuses to do.

While it is very much a romantic melodrama, *Children* also goes to the core of the challenged person's relationship with society and the rights and respect that physically challenged people deserve. Sarah chooses not to speak or read lips, she tells James, because that is what society expects her to do. Signing is something uniquely hers, and those who want to communicate with her can do it her way or not at all.

(Note to parents: *Children of a Lesser God* is rated R for infrequent profanity and relatively demure sexual content that do not detract from the movie's value as a commentary on hearing-impaired individuals.)

Dealing With Physical Deformity

One thing that stands out with these movies is that the filmmaking community is extremely appreciative of performances by actors playing physically challenged characters. Of the eight films mentioned, each of them (except the Australian production *Tim*) resulted in either an Oscar award or nomination for its "handicapped" star. The Oscar winners were Cliff Robertson (*Charly*), Dustin Hoffman (*Rain Man*), Patty Duke and Anne Bancroft (*The Miracle Worker*), Jane Wyman (*Johnny Belinda*), and Marlee Matlin (*Children of a Lesser God*). Unsuccessful nominees were Audrey Hepburn (*Wait Until Dark*) and Alan Arkin (*The Heart Is a Lonely Hunter*), nominated the year Robertson won for *Charly.*

For sheer acting brilliance, however, no performance can match that of Daniel Day-Lewis as the Irish painter and writer Christy Brown in *My Left Foot* (1989). Born with cerebral palsy and unable to control his vocal cords or any other part of his body except his left foot, the indomitable Christy simply refuses to become one of society's invisible misfits.

Christy fights back, learning to write, draw, and speak. He is witty, profane, and violent, a short-tempered fighter and serious drinker. There is no self-pity in Day-Lewis's portrayal of Christy and no pointless rage against his physical limitations. His contempt is saved for those who embrace him as "a crippled genius" but refuse to accept his emotional self. The movie's central irony is that those who do accept the whole Christy are themselves social and economic cripples — his brothers, sisters, and neighbors in the grim, working-class precincts of wartime Dublin.

With its heartrending message about familial bonding and infinite parental love, *My Left Foot* is a glorious family movie. Christy's story, which begins in childhood (with Christy played by the gifted Hugh O'Conor), immediately captures the imagination of young viewers. At the movie's center is Day-Lewis's Oscar-winning performance, an astonishing physical and intellectual achievement. While it is rated R for infrequent profanity and moderate sexual discussions, parents should consider sharing this movie with their children.

Another factor that distinguishes *My Left Foot*'s Christy Brown from the characters previously described — and Day-Lewis from the other actors — is that he is not presented as being conventionally Hollywood-handsome and must suffer physical deformity together with his physical limitations. One reason films about sightless and deaf persons are so popular in Hollywood, of course, is that their "handicaps" are invisible to the eye and they can be safely played by any glamorous leading man or woman.

An even more extreme case of physical deformity than Brown's is found with the character of California teenager Rocky Dennis (Eric Stoltz) in the wonderfully heartwarming *Mask* (1985). Rocky suffers from a rare genetic disorder in which abnormal calcium deposits have caused his skull to continue growing, reaching such hideous proportions that strangers believe at first glance that he's wearing some outlandish Halloween mask.

But Rocky, like Christy Brown, is a battler, and his most effective weapons are humor, charm, and the ferocious intelligence that earns him top academic honors at his public high school. People are initially repelled by Rocky's appearance, and part of his winning grace is that he understands their repulsion and can casually disarm it in an instant. He desperately wants real emotional love, however, and eventually finds it — total and unquestioning — in the most logical place of all, with a young blind girl (Laura Dern).

Mask is a wonderful family drama that not only avoids cliches but challenges and contradicts a few. Rocky's best friends, for example, are the black leather-clad members of a hell-raising motorcycle gang, who happily accept him for the great kid he is. And Rocky's mom (played by Cher) is a drug-taking, sleep-around social outcast who would be conventionally considered a "loser" in almost every sense of the word but one – no mother ever loved her son more than she.

(Another outstanding drama of a physically deformed man's struggles with social acceptance is *The Elephant Man,* filmed in 1980 and set in turn-of-the-century England.)

Dealing With Sudden Disabilities

The challenging new world of the suddenly disabled is a Hollywood staple that has most frequently found expression in features about wounded war veterans. Included in this list are *The Best Years of Our Lives* (1946), with Harold Russell, who did lose his arms in combat, playing a physically challenged man readjusting to peacetime society; *The Men* (1950), featuring Marlon Brando (in his debut film) as an embittered paraplegic patient in a veterans hospital; and the wheelchair-bound Vietnam veterans played by Tom Cruise in *Born on the Fourth of July* (1989) and Jon Voight in *Coming Home* (1978).

A very different kind of story is told in *The Other Side of the Mountain* (1975), where the suddenly afflicted character is a champion skier who suffers a crippling spinal injury in her final tryout run for the 1956 U.S. Olympic ski team. After a period of self-pity, Jill Kinmont (Marilyn Hassett) rallies and determines to perform a valuable social role as an elementary school teacher – only to find that paraplegics and quadriplegics (Kinmont's case) are barred from public school employment.

Too much a contrived melodrama to be wholly effective, *Mountain* – based on a true story – nevertheless paints a convincing picture of a world-class athlete suddenly robbed of the attributes that define her life. As she struggles to create a dramatically different sense of self-worth, a polio-stricken friend gives her some advice that is a central truth of all these films on physical and mental challenges: "There's only one thing that kills cripples, and that's taking themselves too seriously."

Westerns

More American films are devoted to wild West settings and subjects than to any other single topic, and for good reason: from the very first story film, *The Great Train Robbery*, to the popular 1990 hit, *Dances with Wolves*, frontier legends and imagery have informed the whole range of American culture, and, for better or worse, still constitute our most enduring sense of our cultural selves.

It is understandable why this cultural attitude evolved: America was one of the last nations to tame its wilderness and one of the first to translate this experience into popular media forms. In fact, we were still taming the wilderness when motion pictures were in their infancy. *The Great Train Robbery* was made in 1903, nine years before the last western territory, Arizona, gained statehood. Most of the great Western films were made (1945 to 1955), while frontier villages that became the cities of the American West were still less than one hundred years old. Buffalo Bill Cody was a frequent visitor to the sets of early silent Westerns, and the great Western film director John Ford knew legendary sheriff Wyatt Earp personally.

Although other national cultures have powerful, founding myths, only America was blessed with a mythology of high visual impact – and the technology to communicate it broadly and attractively. King Arthur and his Round Table, Hannibal and his elephants, Japan's great samurai warriors – none have so far translated to the screen as successfully and in such numbers as the likes of Billy the Kid and the gunfighters at the OK Corral.

Today the best Westerns still hold our attention with their no-nonsense drama, clear-cut confrontations, and rugged characters. The fantasies they present are those we still yearn to live out, in films, sports, politics, and other facets of our personal and professional lives.

Movies and Myths

The Man Who Shot Liberty Valance (1962) is discussed first here only because the film's summary line could serve as the creative philosophy of all Westerns: "When the legend becomes fact, print the legend." The fact versus legend dispute here involves self-effacing eastern lawyer Ransom Stoddard (James Stewart), newly arrived in the frontier village of Shinbone, and his confrontation with the town's arch-villain, a no-account highwayman named Liberty Valance (Lee Marvin).

Beyond the small central conflict, Liberty Valance has one of the largest canvases of any Western, capturing the old West at a point of transition between the lawless frontier and a civilized society. Idealistic young Stoddard champions the cause of statehood for the territory; the local ranchers oppose it and hire Valance to enforce their will. Between the two sides stands Tom Doniphon (John Wayne), a rancher who realizes the futility of resisting change and comes to Stoddard's support — most importantly in the shootout with Valance. The film is told in flashback, as Stoddard returns from Washington, where he serves as a U.S. senator, to attend Doniphon's funeral.

Liberty Valance is a film comprised of numerous small facets and poignant vignettes, with a sternly humanist moral core and a treasury of colorful supporting characters typical of director John Ford's work: pining ingenue (Vera Miles), stolid European immigrants (Jeanette Nolan and John Qualen), quirky sidekick (Woody Strode), unctuous villain (John Carradine), and wacky old coot (Andy Devine). It upholds the virtues of tolerance, education, friendship, humility, and self-sacrifice and is altogether a treasure of a movie.

Shane (1953) champions the legend of the lone drifter as an avenging angel, appearing as if by divine intervention to take up the cause of the righteous underdog in a life-or-death battle. Here Alan Ladd's title character eases into the middle of a rancher-homesteader confrontation over grazing rights, reluctantly agrees to become involved, sets matters right, and then rides off toward the distant horizon — followed by one of the most famous final lines in movie history.

Shane is told through the eyes of the young son (Brandon DeWilde) of a home-steading couple. The boy is an innocent fully capable of believing in miracles, and his perspective only serves to heighten the ascension of legend over fact. But there is a hard reality at the core of *Shane:* the frequently bloody and bitter dispute between the cattle ranchers — accustomed to having vast unclaimed tracts for grazing their herds — and the later-arriving farmers, armed with govern-ment deeds and intent on putting down roots in the "open-range" prairie.

(Director George Stevens followed *Shane* three years later with the epic *Giant,* which switches to the rancher perspective in siding with a Texas cattle baron against a twentieth century-style sodbuster — the oil wildcatter — thus bringing Western mythologizing up to date.)

The two basic elements of frontier myths were dominion over the land (and the victimized Native Americans who inhabited it) and survival of the natural elements.

Since most Westerns were action-adventure movies, they focused on forceful dominion. *Heartland* (1979) is the antithesis – a quietly intense account of settlers surviving disease, poverty, and despair in making their home in an inhospitable environment. It also could flippantly be viewed as an insight into what the homesteaders in *Shane* did when not fighting range wars or barroom brawls.

Based on first-person journals, *Heartland* follows frontierswoman Elinor Stewart (Conchata Ferrell) as she leaves Denver following her husband's death and takes her young daughter to Wyoming, where she has signed on to keep house for a bachelor rancher (Rip Torn). Elinor intends, in time, to save enough money to buy her own spread. *Heartland* is the story of mother and daughter's first winter on the high plains, an experience that swings between a grinding battle to endure hardship and the growing realization of the depths of love that exist in the extended community now surrounding them.

Red River (1948) presents the legend of the cattle drive as a symbol of the American work ethic and, through it, the humble foundation of great Western personal fortunes. *Red River*'s main character, Tom Dunston (John Wayne), is depicted as an unsympathetic tyrant who literally whips and goads his cowhands into continuing an arduous, long-distance cattle drive until his adopted son (Montgomery Clift, in his film debut) leads a revolt, banishes the old man, and takes over the drive.

The drive itself is undertaken for dire economic reasons, as cattle markets have vanished in post-Civil War Texas and the distant terminals of the new transcontinental railroad offer the only viable opportunity for Dunston to sell his huge herd. Using an old Indian trail (known in Western folklore as the Chisholm Trail) as their route, Dunston's crew sets off on a weeks-long overland trek (the plot borrows freely from *Mutiny on the Bounty*) whose rigors can be eased only by blind obligation to work.

High Noon (1952) presents the legend of the valiant lawman defending the ramparts of decent civilization against the dark forces of anarchic lawlessness and standing up for right when all around him run for cover. (Clint Eastwood later did a nicely nasty turn on the theme in *High Plains Drifter.*) Western sheriffs may not have been paragons of virtue – many, in fact, had a disreputable past – but they are always seen in legendary terms as being ready to put their lives on the line, asking little in return.

Filmed in black-and-white and only 85 minutes long, *High Noon* tells a story that is as stark and simple as the unambiguous moral message it conveys, a Wild West variation on Benjamin Disraeli's famous epigram: "All that is needed for evil to triumph is for a few good men to do nothing."

Sheriff Will Kane (Gary Cooper), about to ride off into retirement with his new bride (Grace Kelly), learns that an evil desperado whom he had helped send to prison several years before has just been released and is returning, bent on revenge, on the twelve o'clock train. Film time and real time are in sync, and *High Noon*'s drama builds as Kane pleads with timid townsfolk to stand with him and the parolee's trigger-happy brothers wait for the train to arrive.

(Career note: *High Noon* was the second of only eleven film roles performed by Grace Kelly, before she abandoned her career to become Princess of Monaco. Two years later, she received a best actress Oscar for *Country Girl,* and her final film was *High Society,* a musical remake of *The Philadelphia Story.*

Sheriff Will Kane was fictional; Wyatt, Morgan, and Virgil Earp were not, and the story of their confrontation with the Clanton boys in Tombstone, Arizona, has been the inspiration for two major motion pictures and for individual scenes in several others. The legend of the OK Corral is a variation on *High Noon*'s showdown between good and evil as a defining moment in American cultural progress, but with significant embellishments having to do with family bonding and community building as the bedrock of frontier survival.

Both *My Darling Clementine* (1946) and *Gunfight at the OK Corral* (1957) concern an event that reportedly lasted less than thirty seconds. Both have also altered the personalities involved, notably that of Tombstone marshal Wyatt Earp, whom history records as a thief, gambler, and drifter who died penniless in Los Angeles in 1929. The makers of these movies, however, were not interested in capturing historical reality but in perpetuating old West legends, and the moral instruction they are presumed to embody. Wyatt Earp and his two brothers represent the civilizing force that tamed the lawless American frontier. They revere their blood bond and their lethal battle against the renegade Clantons symbolizes the triumph of Christian goodness over desert savagery.

The two films are as dissimilar as the real Wyatt Earp and his cinematic recreation. From the swelling sound track to the sweeping VistaVision landscapes, *Gunfight* is a budget-busting Hollywood spectacular, with a sprawling, diffuse story line and star-turn performances by Burt Lancaster as Earp and Kirk Douglas as Doc Holliday, the drunken, consumptive physician-turned-cardsharp who accompanied the Earps to the OK Corral.

My Darling Clementine is quite something else: a spine-tingling black-and-white cinematic jewel in which the dusty frontier is so real you want to shield your eyes from the sunbaked glare. It is one of director John Ford's finest works and features Henry Fonda playing Earp as a quiet, shy, workaday lawman; Victor

Mature atoning for a lifetime of nonsense beefcake roles with a fine performance as Doc Holliday; Walter Brennan working brilliantly against type as the evil Pa Clanton; and Linda Darnell playing Clementine Brown, the girl who follows Holliday out from the East and discovers love with Earp instead.

The Outlaw Josey Wales (1976) has as its text the legend of the wronged innocent pursuing revenge and vigilante justice until all accounts are settled. Rarely, in movies retelling this legend, are the vigilantes punished for their seemingly lawless deeds, it being considered acceptable — within the parameters of the legend — that they are only punishing evildoers and will cease their extralegal behavior when vengeance is taken.

This movie is set during the Civil War in a Southwest no-man's-land. The central character is a simple, uninvolved farmer (Clint Eastwood) whose home and family are wiped out by marauding Union troops. Wales straps on his revolver, sets off alone, and tracks down the killers one by one, in the process becoming the hunted as well as the hunter. This is a plain, unglamorous view of the frontier and its predominantly male population, depicting the civilians as derelict social misfits and the troops as rapacious barbarians.

(Career note: After seven years as cowboy Rowdy Yates on television's "Rawhide," Eastwood went to Italy and starred in three highly entertaining, action-filled "spaghetti Westerns" for director Sergio Leone — *Fistful of Dollars, For a Few Dollars More,* and *The Good, the Bad and the Ugly.* These were basically variations on *Shane*'s avenging angel theme, but with them and a few American-made products — including *Josey Wales,* which he also directed — Eastwood was singularly responsible for keeping the traditional Western movie alive through the culturally inhospitable 1960s and 1970s.)

Western legends weren't only about cowboys and gunfighters. *Jeremiah Johnson* (1972) presents an idealized portrait of a character type unique to the American frontier — the mountain man. At the beginning of the film, young Johnson (Robert Redford) shows up at a bustling riverfront port in the Rocky Mountain foothills, self-exiled from some overly civilized nest. He is there to buy supplies and learn where bear and other game are most abundant. His intention, he announces, is to become a mountain man.

America is a culture rich in mountain men, individuals who have tamed mountains far beyond the bounds of geographic reality in industry, finance, government, education, the arts, and every other field of worthy endeavor. In this context, *Jeremiah Johnson* is an extravagant metaphor for the American experience, a capsule of 350 years worth of restless visionaries setting off into uncharted places, defying skeptics, overcoming great obstacles, and profiting richly from the endeavor. Johnson is not turning his back on civilization but setting out to define a new and, to him, better reality.

The film's spirit is etched in a penultimate line, uttered by Johnson after he has endured struggle, failure, hardship, hunger, the slaughter of his small family, and a grisly battle against hostile Indians. Once again, he encounters the old geezer (played by Will Geer) who had helped him when he was first starting out in the wilderness. "Well, Pilgrim," the old man asks, "were it worth all the trouble?" Johnson responds, "Eh? What trouble?"

While posing as a myth-debunking Western, *Dances with Wolves* (1990) actually speaks directly to one of the central frontier myths — that of the noble savage, the Native American whose land was usurped by white people but whose dignity and rooted nature allowed a centuries-old cultural tradition to endure the intruders' abuses with tribal self-esteem intact. Even though many Western films do indeed paint Native Americans as warlike savages, many also show respect for the natives and draw a careful distinction between peaceful and hostile nations (as does *Dances* itself).

This film's white hero, Lieutenant John Dunbar (Kevin Costner), is also a mythic throwback, with traces of mountain man Jeremiah Johnson and reluctant gunslinger Shane in his makeup. Dunbar is a peripatetic loner who wants to see the frontier "before it's gone" and who rides unafraid and virtually defenseless into the unknown. The Sioux who adopt Dunbar are peaceable but not pacifists, and they have a strong tie to their lush, productive environment — the same environment that vanquishes white intruders, leaving them destitute and suicidal.

Native American Sympathies

Dances with Wolves was not the first Western movie to present positive images of Native Americans, and some of the others are well worth seeking out and viewing for their insights into Native American history and culture.

A Man Called Horse (1970), very much like *Dances with Wolves,* features a bourgeois white man (Richard Harris) in search of himself who finds kinship and self-respect among the Sioux people who adopt him. What's more, he falls in love with a woman of the tribe (an Indian this time, as opposed to the adopted white woman in *Dances*); Native Americans play the Indian characters; and the Indians speak Sioux throughout the movie (their words are translated by a tribesman who was taught English by settlers).

Horse's white hero, an Englishman named John Morgan, is more defiant and unruly than the abject Dunbar, and the Sioux have a pleasantly rough edge, but otherwise the two stories are remarkably similar and the closing scenes virtually identical.

In John Ford's final Western, *Cheyenne Autumn* (1964), the director sought to celebrate Native American culture as an atonement for the negative stereotypes of Indians that cropped up in some of his previous films. As his subject, he selected a legendary incident in Cheyenne folklore: the fifteen-hundred-mile trek by a Cheyenne tribe (one thousand started the journey, and only three hundred finished) from a dismal Oklahoma reservation to their homeland in Wyoming, interrupted by imprisonment at Fort Robinson, Nebraska. The sprawling epic features Richard Widmark as a sympathetic U.S. Cavalry officer and Edward G. Robinson as the educable secretary of the interior Carl Schurz, and makes a farcical detour into Dodge City for some high jinks with James Stewart and Arthur Kennedy as Wyatt Earp and Doc Holliday. Typical of the old Hollywood, director Ford's good intentions are diluted by having the Cheyenne leaders played by non-Native Americans Gilbert Roland and Ricardo Montalban.

Little Big Man (1970), director Arthur Penn's celebrated tongue-in-cheek Western, tells the story of Jack Crabb (Dustin Hoffman), "the sole white survivor of the Battle of the Little Big Horn," over his 111 years of living, loving, and fighting among the Plains Indians. In the course of his remarkably eventful life, Jack is tutored in the gunfighting arts by Wild Bill Hickock, marries a Cheyenne woman, and joins up with General George Custer. While *Little Big Man* takes a long time to say comparatively little, it is redeemed by its passionate empathy with the Native Americans and the majestic performance of Chief Dan George as Old Lodgeskins, the Cheyenne leader whose towering rage at the white man's abuse is the movie's most memorable component.

Tell Them Willie Boy Is Here (1969), based on a true incident that occurred in the summer of 1909, concerns a hot-tempered Paiute Indian (Robert Blake) who kills a tribal elder in a dispute over the man's daughter (Katharine Ross), goes into hiding, and sees his flight transformed into a national emergency by reporters covering a nearby visit by President William Taft. The off-beat story is hampered by writer/director Abraham Polonsky's attempt to use it as a metaphor for his experience with the Hollywood blacklist and also by the film's having to do service as a showcase for emerging star Robert Redford, playing a cynical Anglo sheriff. Despite this baggage, *Willie Boy* is powerful documentation of the harassment suffered by Native Americans who strayed too far – geographically and politically – from their reservations.

Similar to *Willie Boy* in many respects, *Apache* (1954) tells of a fictional warrior named Massai (Burt Lancaster) who refuses to go peacefully when his tribesmen are relocated to a Florida reservation following Apache chief Geronimo's 1886 surrender. Massai hops off the Florida-bound train and forces U.S. lawmen to spend weeks tracking him through the southwestern desert. While Lancaster is no one's idea of a Native American, the film treats the character's cause and culture with a respect impressive for its time.

The best movie treatment of modern Native Americans is the contemporary *Powwow Highway* (1989), a little-known independent production. It features two beaten-down contemporary Cheyenne who battle in different ways to uphold the honor of their people and their legacy. One is a radical Native American activist demanding protection of his people's rights; the other reveres traditional Cheyenne culture, invoking the spirits of departed ancestors and paying obeisance to legendary Native American deeds of the past (including the long trek to Fort Robinson, recounted in *Cheyenne Autumn,* above). This is a witty, educational, and emotionally uplifting movie.

Cowboys Growing Old

When the male action stars of the 1940s and 1950s began to get too long in the tooth and broad in the belly for barroom slug fests and hell-for-leather horse chases, Hollywood did a very smart thing: It produced a remarkable string of movies about cowboys growing old, using their maturity as both metaphor and mirror of changes in America at large. These are not typical Westerns, in as much as the lead characters have a note of irony and reflection that the stars could ill afford in their young-buck roles. Consequently, from their observations and experiences, we learn more about real life than frontier myth.

Hollywood has never been keen on movies that deal with the aging process or the accommodations we make as we grow old. These six films are, therefore, all the more remarkable for dealing unflinchingly with these topics and depicting (in Hollywood terms) elder citizens with respect, reverence, and understanding.

In *Ride the High Country* (1962), two former law-enforcement colleagues (one of them reduced to playing a carnival midway gunslinger) contract to transport a shipment of gold from a mountain mining camp to a bank many miles below. Along the way, they exchange pithy, witty ruminations on life and its meaning and on the overriding value of self-respect. The film stars Joel McCrea and Randolph Scott, the veteran B-Western stalwart here in his last film.

The most contemporary film of the six, *Lonely Are the Brave* (1962), opens with a cowpoke lazing by his campfire and watching a jet plane go keening across the night sky. Star Kirk Douglas, who lists this as his personal favorite among his eighty-plus pictures, plays rowdy, out-of-work cowpuncher Jack Burns, whose world is suddenly being crowded in by jets, shopping malls, and superhighways. Burns is a man one hundred years out of sync (the local police chief calls him "a ghost"), a latter-day Don Quixote doing futile battle against relentless, impregnable windmills and paying a heavy price for his resistance to progress.

Charlton Heston's title character in *Will Penny* (1968) is a Western classic, an aging, unheroic loner scrambling to make a living as a grub line rider in frozen mountain valleys. "Been alone since I was a kid," he says to the woman (Joan Hackett) who befriends him. "Never knew or wanted anything else." Being a loner at fifty is different than being alone at twenty-five, and Heston is brilliant at depicting the pains and pleasures of his burden-of-choice.

Best known as John Wayne's Oscar-winning picture, *True Grit* (1969) is a four-star charmer whose treats include memorable characters, distinctive dialogue, a first-rate plot, and a bang-up finale. But it is most special for Wayne's fine performance as Rooster Cogburn, a legendary federal marshal whose treatment by young Maddie Ross (Kim Darby) should serve as a model of any society's treatment of its elders: his idiosyncracies are indulged; his experience is venerated; his opinions are respected. Indeed, *True Grit* may be the best movie ever produced regarding the frequently testy relationship between aging persons and the younger mainstream of society.

Wayne made two subsequent films that featured variations on his *True Grit* character. The first, *Rooster Cogburn,* is a spurious sequel (costarring Katharine Hepburn) and not recommended. The other, *The Shootist* (1976), is a moving, elegiac drama of an aging gunfighter dying of cancer. While his neighbors see him as a painful anachronism and embarrassing impediment to progress (the year is 1901), Wayne's John Books resolves to prove his mettle, refusing to slip away quietly in a drug-induced stupor. Although not the equal of *True Grit* for overall quality, *The Shootist* resonates on a personal scale: Wayne himself was dying of cancer at the time he made the movie, and this would be his final film.

Actor Richard Farnsworth is not a star of the Wayne-Douglas-Heston magnitude, but his performance as the incorrigible bandit Bill Miner in *The Grey Fox* (1982) is worthy of high praise. The splendid, moody film — also set in 1901 — opens with Miner released from prison after serving thirty-three years for robbing stagecoaches. Stagecoaches don't run anymore, of course, but this is only a passing inconvenience for the resourceful Miner. Trains will do nicely, thank you. A man has to change with the times, and Miner's transition is one of the drollest, career-switch dramas ever put on film.

The continuing popularity of entertainment media whose subject matter is the entertainment industry itself confirms that we are a nation of insatiable voyeurs when it comes to the inner workings of show business. Television programs such as "Entertainment Tonight," magazines such as *Entertainment Weekly,* and newspapers' increasing coverage of the entertainment world all testify to our hunger for the inside scoop on the people who aspire to entertain us.

But the popularity of these media is not a new phenomenon. Movie fan magazines had their heyday in the 1940s and 1950s, while gossip columnists such as Hedda Hopper and Walter Winchell held make-or-break power over Hollywood and Broadway well back into the 1930s.

Moviemakers themselves have long catered to our interest in show biz by turning out numerous behind-the-scenes films featuring various entertainment media settings and presuming to show us how these worlds really work. In fact, the most famous of all backstage dramas, *Phantom of the Opera,* has been the subject of no fewer than five film versions (none of them of any special note).

The following films were selected for the variety of performing arts venues presented, as well as for the quality of the movies included.

Various Backstage Views

The lower depths of show business, far away from the rich-and-famous life-styles, are captured with loving care in Woody Allen's fetchingly surreal comedy *Broadway Danny Rose* (1984). Danny (played by writer/director Allen) is a much-loved, overly devoted agent and manager with a stable of misfit performers that includes a blind xylophonist, a one-legged tap dancer, and a troupe of ice-skating penguins.

But "the greatest Danny Rose story of all," say his friends at the Carnegie Deli, who provide the film's narration, involves a hard-drinking lounge singer named Lou Canova (Nick Apollo Forte), his gum-popping girlfriend Tina (Mia Farrow), and some maladroit mobsters who think it was Danny – instead of Lou – who stole Tina from her gangster fiance. The Danny-Lou-Tina adventure is then played out against a backdrop of small-club striving, in what many consider to be Allen's most finished and accomplished comic work.

In country music, the best backstage look is afforded by *Nashville* (1975), director Robert Altman's highly regarded combination of traditional musical and barbed social satire. Released in large part as a commentary on the 1976 bicentennial hoopla, Nashville uses the country music scene as a microcosm of a two-hundred-years-old America – a nation where the culture clashes first glimpsed in the 1960s have reached into every corner of the populace, affecting the nation's political life as well as its social and cultural activities.

But Nashville is only superficially a political movie. Its real value comes from the insights into the competitive pressures, personality conflicts, and clashing value systems found backstage in this part of the music industry. The several singers represented (said to be based on such real-life performers as Loretta Lynn and Hank Snow) embody a range of musical styles, from black gospel to rhinestone cowboy, from the pure of heart to the purely manipulative. But they are far more than cardboard cutouts, and their very touching stories, seamlessly interwoven, offer piercing glimpses into this uniquely American entertainment scene.

(Note to parents: While *Nashville* has sufficient profanity, violence, and sexual content to earn it an R rating, this material is relatively minimal and well within the context of the larger story.)

The backstage perspective on musical theater doesn't get any better than that provided by *A Chorus Line* (1985), the film translation of Michael Bennett's stage hit, the longest-running Broadway musical ever. The entire story is played out behind the scenes, as a throng of aspirants try out for a new musical and their number is gradually, and often brutally, winnowed down to a final cast of eight. Along the way, the movie slickly intertwines song-and-dance numbers with intimate scenes of performers talking about themselves, their careers, and their lives on the Broadway musical stage. The film goes a long way in illustrating the sweaty backstage reality behind dancer Fred Astaire's comment "I work very, very hard to make what I do look easy."

Behind-the-scenes life in the legitimate theater is brilliantly portrayed in the greatest backstage movie ever, Joseph L. Mankiewicz's *All About Eve* (1950). This is one of those great black-and-white studio-set films that is fresher and livelier than most contemporary outdoor action pictures. The film's charm is in its boldly venomous look at the polite world of "serious" Broadway theater, as applied through the story of an age-obsessed actress (Bette Davis) unnerved by the challenge of a young fan (Anne Baxter) who becomes her fiercest stage competitor.

A decidedly jollier look at backstage Broadway life is found in the bubbly 1937 comedy, *Stage Door*. Featuring a predominantly all-woman cast, *Stage Door*'s action is largely set at a New York City theatrical boarding house where the usually-battling tenants-of-the-moment include a rich cross-section of aspiring show biz pros. There are the two would-be chorus line dancers (Ginger Rogers and Anne Miller), the sensitive serious actress (Andrea Leeds), the wise-cracking comedienne (Eve Arden), the eccentric debutante (Katharine Hepburn) and the good-kid who manages to be every else's best friend (Lucille Ball).

The cast is notable and superlative, and *Stage Door* is a valuable and still greatly enjoyable time capsule of the Great White Way when it was in its heyday.

Whereas *All About Eve* and *Stage Door* deal with the consequences of celebrity on one scale, Martin Scorsese's outstanding *The King of Comedy* (1983) has quite a different point of view: looking at the cult-of-personality theme from the fan's perspective. Superfan Rupert Pupkin (Robert DeNiro) represents everyone who has ever watched a television performer and thought, "Gee, I could do that." Except Pupkin takes it one step further. When he cannot get an audition with the Johnny Carson-like talk show host (Jerry Lewis) whom he idolizes, Pupkin kid-naps the star and takes him home so that Pupkin can live out his fantasy as the ideal talk-show guest. When Pupkin's zany plot is undone, he must face the consequences of his actions, which are totally unexpected but entirely logical.

Even the three-ring circus has received behind-the-scenes treatment from Hollywood, in Cecil B. DeMille's sumptuous 1952 Oscar winner, *The Greatest Show on Earth.* The movie extravaganza has no plot to speak of, only a halfhearted jumble of silly stories about a gruff circus boss (Charlton Heston), the aerialist bombshell who loves him (Betty Hutton), the trapeze artist who loves her (Cornel Wilde), the elephant rider who loves him (Gloria Grahame), and the elephant trainer who loves her (Lyle Bettger). Best of the lot is James Stewart in an offbeat role as a circus clown running from some dark secret in his past.

But this movie is not about secret lives or sawdust romance. It's about the ritual, pageantry, and life-style of the circus in the days when it was an itinerant nation of glamorous performers and wondrous sights. Now it's just another big-ticket arena attraction, and as *The Greatest Show on Earth* attests, we are none the better for it.

Hollywood on Hollywood

Hollywood is never more entertaining than when it is making backstage movies about itself. In fact, filmmakers have been so taken with their own medium over the years that they have produced at least two dozen significant films that focus on the industry. The subjects range from studio moguls (*The Last Tycoon*) to movie extras (*Day of the Locust*), from mythic stars (*Harlow*) to infatuated fans (*Purple Rose of Cairo*). The attitudes expressed by moviemakers range from one of laudatory self-congratulation (*That's Entertainment!*) to bitter self-contempt (*The Barefoot Contessa*).

The best of these films provide younger viewers with an inside look at the history, processes, and personalities behind the medium that consumes much of our leisure time. The look may not be definitive or entirely honest, but in the films listed here, the perspective on moviemaking is always fresh, enlightening, and entertaining.

In the beginning, there were silent movies and silent movie stars, and then there were talking movies and some silent movie stars who couldn't talk so well. Here to tell the story is *Singin' in the Rain* (1952), arguably the most popular musical ever made and a spectacular amusement for viewers of all ages.

The film is a good-time goof – a broad satire on moviemaking with a headlong backstage plot involving some lovely people (Gene Kelly, Jean Hagen, Debbie Reynolds, and Donald O'Connor) and one show-stopping musical number after another. But the film also is rooted in Hollywood reality: John Gilbert, for example, was among the real-life silent film stars whose inadequate speaking voice doomed a career in talkies.

The big studios ruled the old Hollywood depicted in *Singin' in the Rain,* and when the studios began to break up in the early 1950s, the independent producer became king – assembling packages on the fly and selling them to the highest bidder. *The Bad and the Beautiful* (1952) is the awful title of a trenchant film that tracks the rise of a B-movie producer (Kirk Douglas) as he uses manipulation and mirrors to create his independent kingdom. Needing to raise money for a desperately needed hit picture, Douglas's character turns to three successful former colleagues – an actor, a director, and a writer – for support. As they ponder his plea, they tell his and their career stories in flashback, and in the process present a thumbnail perspective on Hollywood at a critical watershed juncture.

The most agreeably eccentric picture on this list is Preston Sturges's 1941 satire *Sullivan's Travels,* a film that underscores Hollywood's ongoing love-hate relationship with itself. John Lloyd Sullivan (Joel McCrea) is a popular director of hit movie comedies, who decides it's time for a change of pace, and decides to direct a social-conscience picture as his next project. But first, Sullivan feels he must sample poverty and homelessness firsthand, and sets out across America as a vagrant with ten cents to his name for a taste of the "real world." Director Sturges, meanwhile, is using comical satire to make the point that well-intentioned filmmakers often run the risk of being dangerously removed from their subject matter.

The story of the married star-couple – with one partner's career going up and the other tumbling down – is such a strong and irresistible plot that Hollywood has produced it three times with the same title, *A Star Is Born.* In 1937, the leads were Janet Gaynor and Fredric March; the 1954 version featured Judy Garland and James Mason and added knockout musical numbers; and the 1976 edition starred Barbra Streisand and Kris Kristofferson, switching the setting to the pop music world. While all three versions provide enlightening insight into the pitfalls of marriages between like-professional individuals, the original *Star Is Born* is the best, with the 1954 version close behind (it's a great Judy Garland showcase) and the Streisand-Kristofferson effort highly forgettable.

Another often told tale is that of the forlorn faded star, forgotten by fans and ignored by peers, and most eloquently captured in the title of one famous variation, *Whatever Happened To Baby Jane?* But the hands-down winner in this category, one of the sleekest pictures ever made on any subject, is *Sunset Boulevard* (1950). "You used to be big," says struggling young writer Joe Gillis (William Holden) upon meeting former silent-movie star Norma Desmond (Gloria Swanson). "I am big," Desmond replies. "It's the pictures that got small."

From that point on, their tempestuous relationship affords Gillis (and us) an exquisitely nasty view of a regal early Hollywood, "when they made $15,000 a week and there weren't any taxes." *Sunset Boulevard* may not tell it as it "really was," but the film's swaggering self-assurance convinces viewers of its authenticity. This is summed up in the delicious scene when Desmond, after years holed up in her Hollywood mansion, revisits a soundstage where she once worked and is patronizingly received by one of her former directors (played by real-life director Cecil B. DeMille).

(Career note: William Holden is one screen performer from the 1940s through the 1970s who is especially effective at connecting with today's young audiences. His slick, haughty world-weariness and drop-dead gorgeousness have strong contemporary echoes, and he can be equally effective in powerful melodrama and action-filled adventure films. For other Holden movies of interest for family viewing, see Appendix B.)

Location shooting has been the industry norm since television compelled movies to expand the medium, get out of the studio, and perfect new equipment technologies that made remote work possible. Life on the modern location site is the subject of *Day for Night* (1973), directed by Francois Truffaut and presenting a happily comic catalog of a director's daily traumas – dealing with visibly pregnant actresses, suddenly dead actors, balky cats, and white cars that are too white. Truffaut was the most internationally popular French director of the 1960s and 1970s, and *Day for Night* is one of his most broadly accessible, continually entertaining features.

Tinseltown Takes On TV Land

When network television arrived on the scene in the 1950s and began to threaten Hollywood's entertainment dominance, the movie industry initially disdained the crass commercialism of television the same way that live-theater professionals looked down on the movies for many, many years. Basically, filmmakers treated television as if it wasn't there. Movie actors scorned offers to perform on TV, and early television stars (Lucille Ball, Milton Berle, and others) were dismissed by Hollywood as frustrated film actors and fringe players unsuited to the higher demands of silver screen performance. Meanwhile, talented actors who got their start on television in the 1950s, such as Paul Newman and James Dean, were quickly scooped up by Hollywood, given the star treatment, and never again seen in television land.

When filmmakers have acknowledged television's existence, it has been invariably in the form of cutting satire, designed to lower the boom on the heinous mass-culture following of television. The result is a handful of films such as *Broadcast News* and *Network* (both R-rated) that may say as much about the movies as they are intended to say about television.

Hollywood's first assault on television was *A Face in the Crowd* (1957), and it used heavy artillery indeed. This angry, quick-paced film was created by the team that previously delivered the landmark labor expose *On the Waterfront* — director Elia Kazan and writer Budd Schulberg and features debut performances by future stars Andy Griffith (in a straight dramatic role), Lee Remick, and Anthony Franciosa.

The no-holds-barred story has loutish bumpkin Larry "Lonesome" Rhodes (Griffith) "discovered" in an Arkansas drunk tank, becoming a local radio celebrity, and rapidly rising to national prominence as a folksy network television personality. Rhodes develops lofty political ambitions, as the movie views with alarm the then-emerging link between television, advertising, and politics, and anticipates the arrival of made-for-TV political campaigns.

"I'm not just an entertainer," says the megalomaniacal Rhodes (said to have been loosely based on television star Arthur Godfrey). "I'm an influence, a wielder of opinion, a force."

In the past few years, it has become increasingly common for performers to turn up in both movies and television, and Hollywood seems to have lost interest in the kind of bitter assaults reflected in earlier films.

Rebels with a Cause

A popular image of the motion picture industry is that of a crass, commercial movie machine where depth and substance take a back seat to dollars and cents. It was in Hollywood, after all, where some long ago moviemaker responded to a plea for more serious pictures by saying, "If you want a message, call Western Union."

Despite this legacy, moviemakers have long been infatuated with the character of the rebellious protestor, standing up for his or her beliefs against overwhelming odds. These characters have become even more common in films made since the 1960s, when nonviolent, conscience-driven protest became acceptable social behavior.

Prior to the sixties, movie protests were milder and the protestors more of the impulsive, me-against-the-world variety. For example, in the legendary *Mr. Smith Goes to Washington,* both protest and protestor are so benign, they would barely merit back-page news coverage these days.

The 1960s made protest a fit and worthy subject for film treatment, as popular culture became defined in part by the hot issues of the moment. Given that Hollywood, in an earlier time and in substantially different circumstances, once fostered a blacklist keeping many creative people from working for twenty years or more, this has been a significant industry development.

But for all the change, Hollywood protest films still steer clear of anything radically outside the mainstream and are no place to look for bold or scathing critiques (the 1991 film *J.F.K.* being a notable recent exception). The films in this collection are significant because they elevate the protestors to the status of cultural acceptability. It's all right to care, to get involved, to risk ostracism. Sure, it helps if you're as charismatic as Marlon Brando or as perky as Sally Field, but regardless, these films do present role models for one more way in which lives can be lived.

In *Mr. Smith Goes to Washington* (1939) James Stewart's Jefferson Smith is the backwoods leader of a state boys' club who receives a surprise gubernatorial appointment to a vacant U.S. senate seat. Barely settled in, Smith takes up the cause of establishing a national boys camp on land in his home state that is targeted for development by the political powerbrokers who run his party system and who control his state house patron.

Under the mentorship of an experienced Capitol Hill aide (Jean Arthur), Stewart undertakes an arduous Senate filibuster and wins the legislative battle. Smith – and the movie – might appear hopelessly innocent by contemporary standards, but they are intended to illustrate that one man and a just cause can carry the day against seemingly insurmountable odds. The movie is as valuable now as it ever has been in providing this lesson. (For more on this film, see the discussion of movies about political subject matter.)

While Jefferson Smith makes a conscious decision to go public with his protest and rally the nation behind his cause, saloon keeper Rick Blaine (Humphrey Bogart) in *Casablanca* (1942) carries out his one-man rebellion as a quiet act of steely deception. Blaine must step gingerly through the political land mines of wartime Morocco, and like that country, remain ostensibly neutral, taking care not to offend the ever-present Nazi officers and troops.

But suave, cynical Blaine has a well-informed conscience and a past history of acting on it, as we learn when he is revisited by lost love, Ilsa Lund (Ingrid Bergman). Knowing he would likely have only one chance to make a strong anti-Nazi protest, rebel-in-waiting Blaine spots his opportunity and acts quickly on it, helping Ilsa and her valiant resistance-fighter husband (Paul Henreid) in their flight to freedom.

Marlon Brando's Terry Malloy plays an altogether different kind of rebel in *On the Waterfront* (1954). Brando is a punched-out ex-boxer who wants to make it through another day at a decent wage, happy in his ignorance until he collides with the waterfront unions and labor boss Johnny Friendly (Lee J. Cobb) in an unforgettable conflict.

While his motivation, hobbies (pigeon raising), and boxing past may be unique, Malloy is a classic whistle-blower – the go-along/get-along good-guy who slowly realizes that the evil he sees around him is indefensible, destructive, and ultimately inescapable. Terry voluntarily testifies before a city crime commission investigating union racketeering, and suffers brutal retaliation. But the lesson of

On the Waterfront is that such costs are not only acceptable, they are essential in maintaining a free society.

Women As Rebels

Moving into more recent times, one phenomenon of Hollywood's post-1960s protest-consciousness has been the creation of films in which women are the boat-rockers. The next three films, all produced in the past twenty years, feature three unique female rebels all operating in virtually identical circumstances.

In *Norma Rae* (1979), Sally Field is a divorced mother of two living in a small southern town (once called "company towns") whose economy is dominated by a single huge textile plant. After watching their factory jobs help kill her father and cripple her mother, the heretofore good-ol'-gal Norma Rae teams up with an outside labor organizer (Ron Leibman) and helps unionize the factory workers. *Norma Rae* is an excellent film and offers an excellent performance by Field, as the spunky, reluctant activist struggling to bring order to her own life and improve the lives of her neighbors. It is also the only one of these three films that is entirely fictional.

In *Silkwood* (1984), Meryl Streep plays Karen Silkwood, a divorced mother of two in a small southwestern town whose economy is dominated by a large plutonium production plant. After witnessing harrowing incidents of plutonium contamination, and having been subjected to the debasing "scrub room" experience, Silkwood/Streep helps investigators look into the hazardous work conditions at the plant. More political and gritty than *Norma Rae,* Silkwood is a long and careful film, with superior performances from Streep, Cher (in her first major film role), and Kurt Russell.

In *Marie* (1986) Sissy Spacek plays Marie Ragghianti, a divorced mother of three in Nashville who, through a twist of political fate, is nominated to head the Tennessee State Parole Board. Once there, she learns that high-level state officials are engaged in selling pardons and paroles, and goes public with her story when the governor's office refuses to support her. While as a film, *Marie* leaves a lot of unanswered questions, the movie is important because it is based on a true episode that ultimately landed the governor of Tennessee in jail.

The Milagro Beanfield War (1988) brings the rebel theme full circle, back to the *Mr. Smith* style of benign, upbeat protest films. The issue at hand involves water rights in the arid Southwest and a devious scheme by land developers and their statehouse allies to evict Hispanic landowners from desirable property.

The iconoclast who challenges the scheme, Joe Mondragon (Chick Vennera), is as ingratiating a protestor as Stewart's Jefferson Smith. He is a charming Don Quixote-style rebel who rallies the people of Milagro behind his defiant act of "liberating" water to irrigate his pinto bean crop. The movie is a subtle, forceful testimony to the value of community and the virtue of mutual support when friends and neighbors are threatened. It is also a witty delight that brilliantly captures the rhythms, sights, and sound of Hispanic culture in the American Southwest.

(Note to parents: *The Milagro Beanfield War* is rated R for profanity and violence that are so minimal as to be negligible. This is an important, lively, and entertaining movie that should be suitable for most families.)

Science Gone Amok

Filmmakers looking for a change of pace from flesh-and-blood villains have always happily turned to the invisible, inanimate, and/or incomprehensible for replacements. Most popular among these nonhuman villains are the creations of modern science.

While the character of the mad scientist is a familiar Hollywood cliche, it is mad science itself that more often turns up on-screen. Rarely, in fact, is personal achievement in science presented in a positive light, and not since the 1940s have scientists been featured characters in major films (*Madame Curie* and *Edison the Man*).

Even the recent *The Right Stuff,* with its story grounded in scientific achievement, focuses on the astronauts who benefitted from science while dismissing the scientists themselves as insensitive bureaucrats. The best that other recent films have done is Steven Spielberg's cuddly space scientists (Peter Coyote in *E.T.* and Francois Truffaut in *Close Encounters*) and the unreassuring comic ironies of *Revenge of the Nerds.*

Scientists are not as charismatic as astronauts, and their impersonal creations are too conveniently presented as an evil threat to worry about narrative honesty. Never mind, for instance, that today's movie industry would be lost without computerized production techniques. Computers are still a favorite evil force, whether plunging us toward Armageddon (*WarGames*) or commandeering a spacecraft (*2001*).

But why spoil the fun? We all love to rail against computers, recoil at medical experimentation, and suspect the very worst of any on-screen bubbling test tube. In films, as in real life, the evil that is invisible, inanimate, and incomprehensible is the most feared of all, and the titles discussed here are an excellent cross section of science gone amok, Hollywood style.

Scientific Threats

Archetypal mad scientist Jack Griffin (Claude Rains) discovers how a drug extracted from a rare Indian flower can make him *The Invisible Man* (1933). He uses his new power to terrorize an English hamlet and plots to sell his secret to the highest bidder and make himself rich. Little does Griffin realize that the drug also will make him stark raving mad! The wonderful H. G. Wells story is brought to life with spectacularly spooky special effects and teaches the timeless movie lesson that even learned scientists should not fool around with things they simply don't understand.

(Career note: Since making his film debut in *The Invisible Man,* Claude Rains leant a droll, dapper presence to more than sixty films before his death in 1967. Rarely a leading man, Rains was more commonly found in crucial supporting roles, exuding a worldly cynicism touched by profound compassion and enhancing some of the all-time great films. Among those discussed in this book are *Casablanca, Lawrence of Arabia, Sea Hawk, The Adventures of Robin Hood, Mr. Smith Goes to Washington,* and *The Wolf Man.*)

A killer virus, soon to be known as *The Andromeda Strain* (1971), wipes out a desert town in the southwestern U.S. and threatens all humankind unless scientists can contain its spread and find an antidote. The action, largely confined to an underground military installation, manages to catch us up and carry us along as the lab detectives race against time to identify the rogue microbes. The culprit is a sci-fi staple: the alien disease for which there may be no known earthly cure.

In the film version of Robin Cook's popular novel *Coma* (1978), healthy young people are mysteriously rendered comatose during routine hospital medical procedures and their inert bodies are then shipped off to a high-security clinic. A crusading surgeon (Genevieve Bujold) wants to find out who, what, where, and why, but she is frustrated at every turn by the hospital hierarchy. Finally, she finds out that the patients' organs are being removed at the clinic and auctioned off in international high-stakes bidding, with the highest bidder getting the purloined organs for transplant purposes. How she finds this out constitutes a fine medical mystery.

Atomic Fears

In *The Day the Earth Stood Still* (1951), humans' irresponsible use of atomic energy threatens the universe, prompting a distant advanced civilization to send one of its citizens—an improbably suave alien named Klaatu (Michael Rennie)—down to Washington to warn the world of the impending danger. Naturally, earthlings want to shoot him. To make believers of the skeptics, Klaatu arranges to stop the world dead in its tracks for a few moments at a preannounced time. The skeptics are convinced that he is telling the truth, but they still want to shoot him. Far more responsible than some later antinuclear pictures, this fast-moving adventure will hold special appeal for children, inasmuch as one of the few people to believe Klaatu is a young boy.

Klaatu's fears in this post-World War II drama are prompted by the first use of the atomic bomb, against Japan in the last days of that conflict. For a compelling, well-researched inside look at the building of the bomb—and the way the madness of the project affected the participating scientists and military personnel—see *Fat Man and Little Boy* (1989), starring Paul Newman as the military officer who oversaw the complex, top-secret project, and Dwight Schultz as the scientist who led the bomb-building team.

In *The China Syndrome* (1979), the mad-science threat escalates from atomic to nuclear power, as an accident at a power plant causes core meltdown and threatens to annihilate all living things in the surrounding countryside. The power company wants a whitewash; a guilt-ridden plant engineer (Jack Lemmon) resists and wants to go public with news of the accident. Crusading journalist Jane Fonda learns of the story, and goes to the plant to get the scoop. The film debuted around the time of an accident at the Three Mile Island power plant in Pennsylvania, becoming as topical as the nightly television news.

Computers as Villains

Sharing modern bugaboo honors with nuclear fission is computer technology and the implied threat of a dehumanized world controlled by unfeeling microprocessors. In *WarGames* (1983), computer whiz Matthew Broderick stumbles onto the access code for a U.S. military computer system (known by the initials WHPR and called "Whopper") and begins messing around with a program that ultimately almost lands the United States in World War III. This top-notch suspense film is not always responsible in what it has to say about computers, but it manages to say it with convincing spiritedness.

The best computer-as-villain movie of all is *2001: A Space Odyssey* (1968), which is partially about a mutinous computer that kills crew members and takes over a spacecraft hurtling toward the moons of Jupiter. *2001*'s HAL 9000 computer (voice by Douglas Rain) is an unforgettable screen villain and moviedom's best case yet for going back to the abacus. *2001* is an icy, elusive series of vignettes that begin at the dawn of man, when apes first become tool-using creatures and confront extraterrestrial intelligence in the form of a tall black slab that emits an otherworldly buzz. The trail of the telltale slabs is then brought into the future, to the year 2001. A U.S. lunar team has discovered one of the objects buried deep beneath the moon's surface, and a space mission is dispatched toward the source of the slab's radio signal, near the planet Jupiter.

(The sequel film, *2010,* is comparatively mundane, saying, in effect, "so much for wonder, magic, and mystery," as it literally explains the first film, while adding a couple of new twists to the familiar story of the forbidding monoliths, the renegade computer HAL, and the disappearance of sole surviving Discovery crewman Dave Bowman (Keir Dullea). The two movies together, however, constitute an entertaining sequential epic full of hope and awe, and are highly recommended for family viewing.)

Back to the Ice Age

The final science-gone-amok film to be discussed here, *Iceman* (1984), is singled out because it is a provocative and comparatively little-known film that deals with a scientific fantasy that captures the imagination like no other: establishing contact with supposedly vanished civilizations. When anthropologists discovered the Stone Age Tasaday tribe on Mindanao in 1973 (later hoax charges notwithstanding) and hikers discovered a Bronze Age man frozen in glacial ice in Austria in 1991, the episodes made headlines around the world. *Iceman*'s premise, in fact, is hauntingly similar to the 1991 Austrian experience.

The first forty-five minutes of *Iceman* are as exciting as anything ever seen in a scientific thriller. A team of scientists working for a commercial oil company at a remote Arctic exploration site discover a prehistoric man frozen solid in a block of glacial ice. He's a Neanderthal of the Inuit tribe, twenty-thousand to forty-thousand years old. The team has the body airlifted back to their laboratory, where they bring the man back to life. The cinematic effect is staggering.

The scientists at Arctic Exploration Area #17 want to find out why the Inuit man perished, why they have been able to revive him, and learn of his culture and his language. But science finally goes amok when team leader Shepherd (Timothy Hutton) decides to experiment even further — to establish communication, make close personal contact, and try to effect cultural bonding over the centuries. But even as Shepherd pursues his obsession, it is in the service of intellectual curiosity and a need to know, admirable motives in any movie on any subject.

Courtroom Dramas

Deep in its socially-conscious heart, Hollywood has always been soft on the Great American Democratic Experiment, and nowhere more so than in filmmakers' fevered embrace of the civil libertarian ideal embodied in the U.S. judicial system. Every man shall have his day in court, a jury of one's peers, blind justice, innocent until proven guilty — these cliches are no textbook abstractions for our screenwriters, but basic story line assumptions in dozens of major films.

For Hollywood, as for Richard Widmark's prosecutor at the beginning of *Judgment at Nuremberg,* a court "is more than a courtroom — it is a process and a spirit; it is the house of law." For Hollywood, the courtroom is where human conflicts are equitably resolved, where culprits' true motives are finally revealed, and where falsely accused defendants are able to clear their good names.

Most of the films discussed here were produced in the 1950s, a period of keen despair for Hollywood's liberal intelligentsia. The Eisenhower White House was perceived as a slough of sleepy inactivity; Congress was seen as a tradition-bound club of cranks and old men; and so the courts, led by Chief Justice Earl Warren's Supreme Court, were upheld by liberals as caretakers of the nation's democratic soul. And so Hollywood turned to the judiciary as a source of movie good guys.

These movies use the courts as laboratories for dissecting the human condition and examining society's ills. Consequently, the movies' best courtroom dramas offer an unusual wealth of detail and observation regarding history, culture, personalities, and interpersonal conflict. Moreover, they are among the most thoughtful, intelligent, and responsible movies that Hollywood has made.

A Cross-Section of Legal Cases

The finest of the classic courtroom dramas listed here is *Anatomy of a Murder* (1959), a highly controversial film, upon its release, due to a realistic, frankly detailed legal perspective on the issues of rape and carnal knowledge. It was also a very popular and much-honored film, receiving an Oscar nomination for best picture and three more for its lead actors.

James Stewart gives one of his best performances as an underachieving small-town lawyer who rises magnificently to the challenge when asked to defend an Army officer (Ben Gazzara) accused of murdering the man who assaulted his wife (Lee Remick). Opposite Stewart, as the young state prosecutor, George C. Scott uses one of his early film appearances to all but steal the movie from his veteran costar.

(Career note: James Stewart is considered by many to be the finest actor in talking motion pictures, and his presence in several all-time great movies discussed throughout this book is testimony to his stature. Several of Stewart's films – *It's a Wonderful Life, Harvey, Rear Window* – are surefire winners with young people, making him an ideal performer through whom to begin introducing youngsters to older classic films. For more Stewart pictures of interest for family viewing, see Appendix B.)

Whereas the trial in *Anatomy of a Murder* is played against a background of small-town ordinariness, the trial in *Inherit the Wind* (1960) represents one of the most sensational courtroom confrontations in American history. This was the 1925 Scopes "monkey trial," pitting liberal legal activist Clarence Darrow against populist fundamentalist William Jennings Bryan on the question of whether a Tennessee schoolteacher could lecture on Darwin's theory of evolution in the face of a state law forbidding the teaching of anything but biblical creationism. This is a caring, patient treatment of a dispute that goes to the core of legal, social, and religious beliefs, lovingly captured by director Stanley Kramer. Spencer Tracy plays Darrow and Fredric March is Bryan, with the courtroom dialogue drawn straight from court records.

In *Adam's Rib* (1949), Tracy and Katharine Hepburn take their long-running comic battle of the sexes into the courtroom, playing husband-and-wife attorneys suddenly opposing each other in a crime-of-passion assault case. One of the best Tracy-Hepburn comedies, the film is enhanced by thoughtful discussions of sexual equality (this was the 1940s!) and the sublime presence of Judy Holliday as the defendant.

The setting for *Witness for the Prosecution* (1957) is an English courtroom, and the mystery drama is alive with detail about the centuries-old culture and tradition of London's storied Old Bailey and Inns of Court. The story comes from mystery writer Agatha Christie (inspiration for television's "Murder, She Wrote") and is filled with her characteristic twists and turns, here involving a murdered widow, a young rake, and a large inheritance. The stars are Tyrone Power, Charles Laughton, and Elsa Lanchester.

Twelve Angry Men (1957) is not a courtroom drama at all, but a jury room drama. It is also Hollywood's definitive testimonial to the American criminal justice system, with one lone jury member holding out and, through the power of his well-reasoned beliefs, being able to sway his eleven fellows (originally in favor of conviction) to his way of thinking in the trial of a young boy accused of killing his father. The excellent ensemble acting is led by Henry Fonda and includes a handful of players who would carve out significant careers as featured and supporting actors, including Jack Klugman, Lee J. Cobb, and Martin Balsam.

Outside Traditional Courtroom Settings

Judicial process is not confined to traditional courtrooms only, of course, and Hollywood has made the most of this leeway. In *Judgment at Nuremberg* (1961), for example, the setting is a war-crimes tribunal conducted by occupying American forces in Germany following World War II. The film faithfully depicts how such proceedings operated within judicial parameters that were unique in terms of legal history and human drama.

The plot's central concept is brilliant: instead of the usual thuggish Nazi generals, *Judgment at Nuremberg*'s defendants are other lawyers and judges – professional men like the prosecutors themselves – whose alleged crimes were to faithfully execute their nation's laws while serving as officers of the German court. Must judges always blindly enforce the law, or do they have a higher responsibility to defy laws that they feel are unjust? This is only one of the issues raised in the gripping drama, whose powerhouse cast includes Spencer Tracy, Richard Widmark, Burt Lancaster, and Maximilian Schell (an Oscar winner), with knockout cameos by Montgomery Clift, Marlene Dietrich, and Judy Garland. Stanley Kramer is the director.

The nontraditional courtroom setting in *The Caine Mutiny* (1954) is a U.S. Navy court-martial proceeding, and the legal questions concern the responsibilities of men under command to their superiors. The junior officers of the USS *Caine* had become convinced that their imperious commander, Captain Philip Francis Queeg (Humphrey Bogart), was incompetent and had seized control of the ship from Queeg. Now the usurpers must answer for their mutinous actions, setting up a titanic clash of egos and ambition between the well-educated officers and the blue-collar Navy commander Queeg.

Beyond its fascinating personality conflicts, *The Caine Mutiny* is known as a virtual treasury of vintage Bogart moments: the towline-cutting scene, counting the missing strawberries, rolling the ball bearings, and, finally, the self-destructive climatic monologue. It is a masterful performance and a spellbinding film that holds unseemly attraction for young viewers.

(For courtroom drama at the highest levels, see two dramas involving the U.S. Supreme Court: *First Monday in October,* described in the discussion of movies about politics, and *Separate But Equal,* included in the section on race relations.)

Pop Music and Musicians

For most of us, popular music consists of a collection of carefully crafted sounds and images emanating from recordings, videos, television programs, and distant concert stages, with occasional newspaper or magazine articles filling in some real-world background on performers' lives and personalities. Frequently, even the latter are as carefully packaged as their subjects' performances.

Movies dealing with pop music can be of great value in plugging the gaps in our knowledge. At their best, these pictures illuminate the factors contributing to performers' success, the influences on their work, and the historical context from which their music comes — showing, for example, the roots of today's rock and country sounds in earlier jazz, blues, and folk music.

A Musical Microcosm

The American popular music scene was made up of isolated pockets of activity, from Broadway to rural dance halls, until radio and recording technologies emerged in the early twentieth century to help create a truly national culture. No film captures the grand sweep of this transition better than *Yankee Doodle Dandy* (1942), which begins with its featured character — composer-performer George M. Cohan — traveling the nation's vaudeville circuit with his family as The Four Cohans in the late 1800s, and ends in the 1940s, with Cohan a national celebrity, famous for such popular hit tunes as "Mary," "Over There," and "Give My Regards To Broadway."

Yankee Doodle Dandy is one of the best musicals, backstage movies, and family dramas ever made, offering sublime cultural richness and superb technical quality. While the entire cast is exemplary, the film is dominated by the lead-role performance of James Cagney, who switched gears from his popular gangster roles to score one of the great personal triumphs in Hollywood history. Watching Cagney perform the title song sequence is one of the great joys that movies have to offer.

Beyond that, however, *Yankee Doodle Dandy* paints a picture of our popular culture maturing from primitive, homely stage acts to big-budget Broadway spectaculars, where the driving trend is to the newest, freshest, and flashiest. Toward the end of the film, this spirit is captured as a semi-retired Cohan attempts a fruitless dialogue across the generation gap with some youngsters who have stopped by his farm, and who are baffled by the old man's ignorance of their be-bop lingo.

Roots of Modern Music

As a new national popular culture began to take shape in the early 1900s, its growth was fueled by the emergence of strong, visionary personalities who could exploit the new entertainment media and lead mass audiences in creative new directions.

The Glenn Miller Story (1954) presents an entertaining biography of one such innovator, a talented musician-arranger who broke the mold of big-band homogeneity in the 1920s and established a wildly popular personal musical style. The debt that band leader Glenn Miller and other swing band innovators of the period owed to black jazz artists is hinted at when Miller (played by James Stewart) sits in with Louis Armstrong's group in a Prohibition-era jazz club. The film is helped enormously by the timeless appeal of Miller's music, with many of the performers' parts played by real musicians of the era — including trumpeter/singer Armstrong, drummer Gene Krupa, and bandleader Ben Pollack.

(The screen biography of a Miller contemporary and fellow musician-arranger is told in 1955's *The Benny Goodman Story,* starring Steve Allen as the clarinetist-band leader and also featuring a number of real-life jazz artists.)

Big bands of the swing era, such as Miller's, frequently featured female vocalists to give the band a distinctive personality to match their musical style. One of the most popular band vocalists of the era was Ruth Etting, whose story is told in the excellent 1955 film *Love Me or Leave Me.* Etting (played by Doris Day) was a national star in the 1920s and 1930s, beginning her career as a dime-a-dance girl in Chicago, gaining fame with Broadway's Ziegfeld Follies, and touring for several years with an assortment of accompanists. To give the movie some zing, the story focuses on Etting's involvement with Chicago organized crime figures, specifically a leg breaker named Marty "The Gimp" Snyder, and their role in her success in speakeasy supper clubs. While the plot may be a bit outlandish, the presence of archetypal Hollywood gangster James Cagney as Snyder and former big-band singer Day as Etting gives the film more than enough real-world resonance to make it special.

Like Glenn Miller, Bix Beiderbecke was an innovative instrumentalist of the early twentieth century who was deeply influenced by black jazz musicians and who challenged the easy-listening big-band convention of his time. Beiderbecke's story is the basis for the fictional *Young Man with a Horn* (1950), in which hot-licks jazz trumpeter Rick Martin (Kirk Douglas) rebels at being forced to adapt his rip-it-up style to a dance band's schmaltzy sound (Beiderbecke himself played with Paul Whiteman's orchestra in the 1920s).

Young Man with a Horn is a nicely cynical tale, dealing sensibly with the lonely struggles of creative jazzmen without becoming indulgently sentimental. Doris Day again is cast as a big-band singer, while Lauren Bacall plays her rival for Martin's affections, and jazz pianist/composer Hoagy Carmichael, who helped discover Beiderbecke in the 1920s, plays a character very much like himself. Douglas's trumpet parts were recorded by Harry James.

Black Influences

By and large, the creative and courageous black musicians of the pre-rock era have gotten short shrift in the movie world. Moreover, most of what exceptions do exist cannot be recommended for family viewing due to the prevalence of objectionable material (including profanity, sexual content, and depiction of drug use). These films include *Cotton Club,* set in and around a 1920s Harlem jazz club; *Lady Sings The Blues,* the film biography of Billie Holliday; and *Bird,* the biography of trailblazing black jazz musician Charlie "Yardbird" Parker. Two additional movies that are R-rated and cannot be recommended for family viewing are *Crossroads* about black blues musicians' influence on mainstream popular music and *The Five Heartbeats* the story of a star-crossed black singing group. We mention these movies because to omit them would obviously leave a big hole in our look at popular music through film.

Counterposed against the early big-band and jazz innovators were the traveling folk musicians, who formed a subterranean culture that moved boldly above ground in the 1960s with the coffeehouse folk music boom. This world has been blessed with a great screen treatment in *Bound for Glory* (1976), a film that rises majestically above the typical film biography to capture Depression-era America with painterly elan.

Superficially, this is the story of Woodrow Wilson "Woody" Guthrie, perhaps the most gifted and prolific twentieth-century folk composer ("This Land Is Your Land," "Good Night, Irene," and others). But the film is especially impressive in recreating the social context out of which the American folk tradition grew and in showing how driven folk artists such as Guthrie (played by David Carradine) effectively used music as a tool for union organizing, political protest, and expressing all-purpose outrage. Guthrie was not the first such artist, but he was the most successful at inspiring succeeding generations of performers to use the well-tempered message as part of their musical repertoire (including, of course, Guthrie's son, Arlo).

Like *Bound for Glory, Coal Miner's Daughter* (1980) is notable more for the context it creates around its subject, country singer Loretta Lynn, than for its depiction of the subject herself. The context here is one of struggle and chance, as the movie traces Lynn from her impoverished Appalachian childhood to Grand Ol' Opry stardom and emotional breakdown, detailing the connecting elements between her life and her music. One of the finest of all screen biographies, *Coal Miner's Daughter* features transcendent performances by stars Tommy Lee Jones and Sissy Spacek, who does her own singing in the movie and won the Academy Award for best actress.

Patsy Cline was Loretta Lynn's friend and mentor (in *Coal Miner's Daughter,* she's played by Beverly D'Angelo), and one of the first female country singers to become a national mainstream star before her death in a 1963 plane crash. Cline's own story is told in *Sweet Dreams* (1985), with the primary focus on her tempestuous relationship with her manager-husband (Ed Harris) and her struggle for independence and self-esteem. Jessica Lange plays the lead, with Cline recordings covering the numerous concert scenes.

Snuggled up next to country is western music, a style best personified in the 1970s and 1980s by Texan Willie Nelson. Unlike Lynn and Cline, Nelson himself has acting pretensions and has made a number of entertaining films. One of them, *Honeysuckle Rose* (1980), amounts to an extended Nelson concert film (he's called Buck Bonham here) with a thin, appealing plot that dwells on the sins and joys of touring. The movie's best scenes capture Bonham's Fourth of July picnic, bringing to life the cliche of music as extended-family, with friendship and forgiveness among its highest tribal values. It's a great platform for Nelson and also features an impressive piece of acting and singing by Dyan Cannon, as Nelson's wife.

The Rise of Rock

Country and western and its close relative, black rhythm-and-blues, were among the major influences on early rock-and-roll performers such as Jerry Lee Lewis, whose story is told in 1989's *Great Balls of Fire* (R-rated). While Lewis developed his distinctive sound in rural Louisiana in the mid-1950s, next door in Texas, Charles Hardin "Buddy" Holly was drawing on very similar influences to create a very different kind of rock style. *The Buddy Holly Story* (1978) brilliantly captures these years and that style, and makes the point that, like the swing bands of the 1930s, many breakthrough white rock groups of the 1950s owed a huge debt to black culture.

In fact, *Holly*'s Holly (wonderfully played by Gary Busey) was so influenced by rhythm-and-blues that music business impresarios at first thought his records were the work of black musicians, and his Crickets are depicted here as the first white band ever to play Harlem's Apollo Theater. The cross-over style typified by Holly and the Crickets was a revolutionary music industry marketing concept, and its success helped to make professional life easier for many white and black performers to come.

Rock and roll also owed a heavy debt to Hispanic culture, as is related in the Richie Valens story, *La Bamba* (1987). Valens was the son of migrant field workers who grabbed for the brass ring of 1950s musical success and scored with two national hits — the title song and "Donna" — before perishing in the Iowa plane crash that also claimed the lives of Buddy Holly and J. P. "Big Bopper" Richardson. *La Bamba,* with Lou Diamond Phillips debuting in the lead role, excels at reflecting the energy and cultural integrity of Hispanic music, as well as the excitement of the 1950s rock explosion.

Finally, the seminal figure of 1950s rock, Elvis Presley, is represented on video by several documentaries (the best being the two-volume 1990 collection *Elvis: The Great Performances,* produced by Buena Vista) and by *Elvis,* the outstanding fictionalized treatment of Presley's life originally broadcast as a 1979 made-for-TV movie.

In addition to the expected recounting of the Presley legend, *Elvis* offers a glib psychological profile of a gifted artist who was driven by mother love and the loss of his twin brother, Jesse, who died at birth. It also demonstrates one way to capture a legend on-screen, with actor Kurt Russell's funky, low-key charm helping to paint an appealing portrait of the plain-folk man who became an international legend.

Beatles On-Screen

After the first blistering burst of energy exemplified by the likes of Presley, Lewis, Holly, and Valens, rock-and-roll went into a period characterized by repetition, imitation, and sweet-voiced performers custom-crafted for the broad mainstream. That all changed with the arrival of the Beatles in 1963-64. Youngsters who wonder what the Beatles — and the 1960s — were all about can find the answer in the group's extraordinary first film, *A Hard Day's Night* (1964).

Wild, wonderful, funny, and pounding with a transforming, visceral energy, director Richard Lester's creation is a Beatles concert film disguised as a day-in-the-life docudrama of a rising young British rock band preparing for a television appearance. The movie works on both levels, with the backstage material capturing the phantasmagoric frenzy of pop celebrity and the Beatles' familiar songs packaged in distinctive, narrative settings (a precursor to today's music videos). The Beatles would grow and become better musicians and composers, but *A Hard Day's Night* captures the Fab Four when they were freshly minted as the most powerful pop culture force ever unleashed on the world.

The Beatles made two more films — *Help!* (1965), a more traditional feature film in which the group is pursued by members of a mystical cult whose magic ring has fallen into Ringo's hands, and *Let It Be* (1970), a true documentary that records the making of the band's final album and signs off with a spontaneous London rooftop concert that was to be the Beatles' last public appearance together.

The best "Beatles movie" of all may be one that band members had little to do with. An animated feature produced in 1968 and directed by George Dunning, *Yellow Submarine,* not only perpetuates the Beatles' magic but also evokes the whimsical fantasy that swirled around so much of 1960s culture. The film features four cartoon characters based on John, Paul, Ringo, and George, along with a few original Beatles' songs, but the Beatles reportedly did not actually work on the film and there was a question, right up to the film's release, as to whether they would have any official association with it.

Fortunately, they did, and *Yellow Submarine* is one of the great pop culture treasures of the 1960s. It depicts a magical trip to a place called Pepperland, where the four mop-topped lads come to the rescue of the local Pepperlanders in fighting off ogres called the Blue Meanies. It's a frolicsome delight of elegant wordplay and dumb physical fun that is guaranteed to amuse children of all ages.

Rites of Passage

The phrase "rites of passage" refers to those life-defining events that profoundly alter who we are, and provide us with the kinds of emotional and/or physical experiences that can set our lives on new courses, taking us from one stage of personal growth to another. Usually, these "passages" are accompanied by a heightened awareness of our place in the world and a deepened appreciation of the human condition.

Strictly speaking, such experiences can happen at any time in our lives, as no one ever truly stops learning and growing. We might expect this to be reflected in our popular culture, but in movies, "rite of passage" stories most commonly concern the experiences of young people.

Over the past thirty years these films have been driven more by Hollywood economics than creative inspiration drawn from real-world experiences. As movie-makers discovered that huge hits can be made through repeated business of young filmgoers, they began exploiting this market with superficial "passage" movies that unquestioningly took their young protagonists' point-of-view in confronting the adult world.

This may have generated excellent box-office revenues, but it also produced a school of movies in which reality is corrupted and moral instruction is nonexistent. On the other hand, further back in time, movies were no better, only different. Before 1960, we typically find movies treating youngsters as little more than adults-in-waiting, with no explicit emotional or philosophical agenda worthy of grown-ups' attention.

It is difficult, therefore, to find rite-of-passage movies striking the perfect balance between objectivity and compassion, making them both entertaining and instructive. The following films are selected because they come as close as any in doing this, and because they present different kinds of young people, at different ages, from different backgrounds, experiencing a variety of changes.

Among the most popular rites-of-passage themes is that of young innocents suddenly thrust into alien circumstances and forced to adapt to new ways of living. A classic Hollywood rendition of this theme, *Captains Courageous* (1937), deals with an extreme set of circumstances, and is all the more effective for shaping a compelling human melodrama out of material that could have been infantile and sentimental. A spoiled rich kid, played by child star Freddie Bartholomew, is accidentally swept off the deck of a transatlantic ocean liner and is then pulled from the water by the crew of a fishing vessel off the New England coast.

At first, the youngster believes that his tales of his family's great wealth and power will have the poor, hard-working Portuguese fishermen falling over themselves to help whisk him quickly back to port. Instead, they refuse to alter their schedule and insist that he become a fully functioning member of their crew, working alongside everyone else during the several weeks remaining on their fishing trip. Among those educating the young man to respect and appreciate his fellows are trawler Captain Disko Troop (Lionel Barrymore) and the crew's best fisherman, Manuel (Spencer Tracy, in an Oscar-winning performance).

Sometimes the change in culture can be so appealing that the youngster has no desire to return to his former life. This theme is frequently employed to draw contrasts between so-called civilization and pagan cultures, usually for the purpose of reminding modern people of the essential goodness they have abandoned in climbing upwards from a primitive past.

An interesting use of this theme is found in *The Emerald Forest* (1985), and its story of an American civil engineer, working in the Brazilian jungle, whose young son is kidnapped by a tribe known as "The Invisible People." The son comes of age as the movie progresses, adapting to life among the tribesmen, while his father spends ten years searching for the boy. Although the movie spends more time focused on the father's search than the son's experience (and the whole movie descends into a lame shoot-'em-up at the end), the passages concerning the boy's life among the rain forest tribesmen are remarkably effective and moving.

A reverse spin on this story is found in William Golding's celebrated novel, *Lord of the Flies,* which was made into a movie on two occasions (1963, 1990). Here a group of supposedly "civilized" young boys suddenly find themselves thrust into primitive conditions when they are marooned on a tropical island. A number of them quickly revert to savage ways, complete with pagan rituals, while the more sensible among them are repulsed by this development and fight to preserve some semblance of civilized order.

The first, 1963, film version of the book is not only a better production than the 1990 "modernized" version, but is also more suitable for family viewing (although the minimal-but-disturbing violence might make it troubling for younger children).

A variation on the alien-circumstance theme is that of the young innocents who are suddenly thrown into roles traditionally fulfilled by adults, as happens to the eleven boys who star in one of the most attractively offbeat Westerns ever made, *The Cowboys* (1972). The youngsters here are excused from school in their Montana frontier village in order to help a local rancher (John Wayne) drive his cattle herd to market, after the hired hands catch gold fever and head off to mining territory.

The Cowboys is an exciting adventure tale, unfortunately marred by a violent ending. Otherwise, it's a great way to introduce young viewers to the glory of movie Westerns and for them to watch how these youngsters grow and mature during their time on the trail.

A dramatically different context is presented in the film version of Betty Smith's popular novel, *A Tree Grows in Brooklyn* (1945), a coming-of-age story set in turn-of-the-century New York City. The main character is a bright, creative teen-ager named Francie (Peggy Ann Garner) who is so eager to get a quality education that she's reading her way through the authors in the local public library, from A to Z.

If Francie has a flaw, it is in her unthinking idolatry of her father Johnny (James Dunn), a singing waiter known as the "Brooklyn Thrush." Johnny is a devoted, charming father, and Francie loves him dearly, despite his weakness for alcohol and outlandish dreams of fame and fortune. In part because of her father's irresponsibility, Francie must eventually give up her cherished schooling and work to help support her impoverished family — compelled to become an "adult" much sooner than she expected or hoped.

Yet another context is offered in *Sounder* (1972), the story of the young son (Kevin Hooks) of an impoverished sharecropper in the depressed rural Louisiana of 1933. When his father (Paul Winfield) is jailed for stealing meat for the family's table, the boy, David Lee, must help his mother (Cicely Tyson) provide for the family.

David Lee eventually leaves home in search of the prison camp where his father is being held. Along the way, he meets a kindly schoolteacher (Janet MacLachlan) who uses books and writers to introduce the youngster to the exciting world at large. *Sounder* (name of David Lee's faithful dog) is an exceptional family film that offers vivid characters and a story that is sensitive, enlightening, and compassionate.

Dealing With Loss

Perhaps the most common rites-of-passage theme of all is the challenge young people must face when dealing with loss – through death or prolonged absence – of a friend, parent, or other loved one.

In the popular Swedish film, *My Life as a Dog* (1985), twelve-year-old Ingmar (Anton Glanzelius) moves in and out of orphanages as his single mother battles financial hardship and physical debility, struggling unsuccessfully to keep her family together. Finally, Ingmar moves from his city home to live with relatives in a rural town, and must cope with the loss of his mother as well as his social isolation.

The young girl in Carson McCullers' *The Member of the Wedding* (1952) has already lost her mother when the movie opens. Her emotional support is provided by her neighbor-cousin (Brandon DeWilde) and her father's black housekeeper (Ethel Waters). Nonetheless, twelve-year-old Frankie (Julie Harris) feels that she's "a member of nothing in the world, an unjoined person," and lives for the day when her soon-to-be-married brother (Arthur Franz) and his new bride will take her away and give Frankie a real home. Ultimately, Frankie must deal with yet another great loss and learn that she must make her emotional peace with the world entirely on her own.

The loss suffered by the young prep school students in *Dead Poets Society* (1989) is both personal and intellectual. First they experience the loss of a fellow student and then must watch helplessly as the school callously dismisses the English teacher (brilliantly played by Robin Williams) who has inspired them to "make your lives extraordinary." *Dead Poets Society* is notable for dealing forthrightly with the transitory quality of life, and the value of maintaining one's integrity in the pursuit of personal goals – not living to please others.

Fallen Idols

Another kind of loss and coming-of-age experience is found in films dealing with young people coming to grips with the decline and fall of individuals whom they have previously looked up to.

In the modern Western *Hud* (1963), the story is about a teenage boy (Brandon DeWilde) who idolizes his tough, cynical, carousing uncle (Paul Newman). As the story unfolds, however, young Lon realizes that Uncle Hud is less than meets the eye: Hud's cynicism masks a deep cruelty and his goodtime demeanor is an excuse for irresponsibility. Almost too late, Lon realizes that the better role model is his stern, seemingly inflexible rancher-grandfather (Melvyn Douglas).

The fallen idol in *The Mosquito Coast* (1986) is the crazed, charismatic inventor and father Allie Fox (Harrison Ford), whose railing against modern society finally prompts him to uproot his family from their comfortable American home to establish a new life in the Central American jungle. His children are in awe of their father as he creates a perfect community in the wild, making peace with both the forbidding tropical environment and its native inhabitants.

The children's feelings toward Allie begin to change dramatically, as his impulsiveness puts the family at great risk and his antisocial ranting becomes increasingly violent. The gradual, inevitable unravelling of the Fox family unit is spellbinding, and Ford's performance as the source of its destruction is masterful.

(Note to parents: Both *Hud* and *The Mosquito Coast* are films of exceptional quality, and highly suitable for family viewing. Because of their intense, emotional subject matter, and their frank treatment of bitter reality, some parental caution is advised.)

Youth in Wartime

Films about armed conflict have traditionally been used, in whole or in part, to present a unique context for rites-of-passage drama. Most of these films deal with battle combatants themselves, and none better than *Red Badge of Courage* (1951), based on the Stephen Crane novel. A brief (69 minutes), pungent, unforgettable film, *Badge* follows a young Union soldier (Audie Murphy) through his first few days of training, a long winter of waiting, and finally into his baptism of fire.

It is giving nothing away to say that the boy-soldier thinks his regiment is hopelessly outnumbered in this first encounter, and flees the battlefield, later learning that his comrades actually fought off the Confederate Army assault. "He performed his mistakes in the dark, so he was still a man," the narrator (James Whitmore) tells us, as the soldier returns to the front lines and performs with bravery. In addition to being a memorable rite-of-passage film, *Red Badge of Courage* is also one of the finest films ever made at dramatizing the sheer personal terror of warfare, together with the spirit of men-under-siege camaraderie that binds the troops.

The perspective in *Hope and Glory* (1987) is the opposite of *Red Badge of Courage* and most other war movies: that of war's victims. The film opens in September 1939 with the central character, a small boy named Billy (Sebastian Rice Edwards), living with his family in London. When the Germans invade Poland, Britain declares war and, says the boy, "nothing would ever be the same again." The rest of the film follows young Billy, his family, and his pals, as they cope with the reality of warfare in the form of absent fathers, shortages of food and clothing, and continual bombardment of their neighborhoods.

The same perspective in the same war is adapted in another fine film, set on the opposite side of the world from *Hope and Glory*. The young British boy (Christian Bale) in *Empire of the Sun* (1987) is the son of an English merchant in Shanghai at the start of the Pacific War, when the Japanese move ruthlessly to take control of China and drive out or capture all foreigners. The boy ends up in a Japanese prison camp, and the four years covered in the film, 1941-45, see him mature from a spoiled, dreamily defenseless child to a mature survivor. It is a dramatic, believable transformation, depicted within the context of epochal world events (in which the Japanese are not always portrayed as evil villains).

Deeper Awakenings

In recent years, with the liberation of the movie rating system, many successful rites-of-passage films have dealt with young people's social and sexual awakening. By the very nature of this subject matter, few of these films can be deemed wholly suitable for family viewing and are better left to the individual discretion of parents. The following three are among the more acceptable – although parents may still want to check them out first.

Based on a William Faulkner story, *The Reivers* (1969) is set in rural Mississippi and concerns typical Faulkner characters – lowlife "swamp rat" Boon Hogenbeck (Steve McQueen), his fun-loving black buddy Ned McAsland (Rupert Crosse), and wide-eyed, ready-for-life Lucius Binford (Mitch Vogel). One summer day in 1905, Boon and Ned give young Lucius a taste of the real world by driving to the big city of Memphis where Lucius is introduced to such cosmopolitan phenomenon as "ladies of the evening," horse-race gambling, and shady law-enforcement officers. It's all executed with good taste, and the movie is an all-around charmer.

American Graffiti (1973), George Lucas's pre-*Star Wars* film, captures the restless, combustible energy of early 1960s American youth. Lucas's film takes place over several hours on a late summer's evening, as the youth of the generic California suburban town cruise the local "strip" looking for any kind of action that will give some spark to their largely aimless lives. The movie unfolds in a series of vignettes, most of them humorous and all of them perceptive in their insights into a variety of youthful social situations and personality types — from college-bound preppies to rowdy bikers.

Breaking Away, a sleeper hit of 1979, is an utterly delightful and highly recommended film focusing on four recent high school graduates trying to figure out what to do next in life. The most ambitious among them (Dennis Christopher) persuades the others to join him in entering a long-distance bicycle race against teams of local college boys.

But in addition to being formidable race opponents, the collegians also symbolize the more worldly social forces who have traditionally made life miserable for townies like the movie's heroes. The climactic race, therefore, becomes the ultimate double-edged challenge of "breaking away."

Meet the Press

Hollywood's depiction of journalists has turned 180 degrees in the past few years. Once stereotyped as hard-drinking layabouts and flunky hacks, journalists are now presented as heroes and role models in important films about important subjects.

As evidence, consider how newspapermen were described by a character in the 1930s film *Nothing Sacred:* "The hand of God reaching down into the mire couldn't elevate one of them to the depths of degradation — not by a million miles." Today we see megastars such as Mel Gibson, Robert Redford, and Sally Field cast as glamorous reporters who are paragons of integrity and virtue. In addition, it has become common for films to feature journalists as lead characters, as journalism has become a favorite Hollywood means of viewing world events (such as the antiapartheid struggle in *Cry Freedom,* and the Latin American revolution in *Under Fire*).

Many films featuring reporters are written by exjournalists and so provide an unusually deep and authentic look into the profession. Through them we gain a keen appreciation of the forces and issues at play in the world of print and electronic media and how the participants deal with these forces.

A popular journalism tale is told in *The Front Page,* a rip-roaring comedy written for the stage by Charles MacArthur and Ben Hecht (an ex-newspaperman) and committed to film a total of four times. The preoccupation of all four movies is the same: the clash of personal and professional values, as told through the battle of wits and wills between *Morning Post* publisher Walter Burns and his ace reporter, Hildy Johnson, who is soon to be wed and moving on to work in a new career with fewer hassles and higher pay.

The Front Page was first filmed in a flamboyant 1931 version starring Adolphe Menjou and Pat O'Brien and remade in 1974 with Jack Lemmon and Walter Matthau. In 1940, screenwriter Hecht rewrote the story by transforming the part of Hildy Johnson into a woman's role. The result, *His Girl Friday,* is one of the all-time great screen comedies (starring Cary Grant and Rosalind Russell) and a highly recommended family treat. (The same story line was used in 1988's *Switching Channels,* starring Burt Reynolds and Kathleen Turner, with the setting moved to television and the result a dismal bore.)

Hecht was also the screenwriter for *Nothing Sacred* (1937), a darkly satirical comedy that zeroes in on reporters' gullibility and susceptibility to fraud in their pursuit of an exclusive story. A rustic lovely from tiny Warsaw, Vermont (Carole Lombard), whom the public believes to be dying of radium poisoning (she knows differently), is brought to New York by a crusading reporter (Fredric March) and becomes the doom-swathed toast of Gotham.

The most celebrated journalism film of all time, frequently topping lists of the greatest movies ever made, is *Citizen Kane* (1941), written by and starring Orson Welles. This film is based on the career of publishing titan William Randolph Hearst, whose newspapers refused to carry advertising for the movie on its release. Welles's story of Charles Foster Kane, breathtaking in its narrative sweep and cinematic style, dramatizes the foundation of a great newspaper empire on the basis of corruption, greed, and megalomania.

It was not only powerful publishers who built their journalistic careers on shaky moral foundations; *The Sweet Smell of Success* (1957) explores the shadowy side-streets of journalism traveled by newspaper gossip columnists dealing in blind items and bald rumor. This movie is set in the New York of the 1950s, a time when real-life columnists such as Walter Winchell held make-or-break sway over show business careers. It focuses on malevolent columnist J. J. Hunsecker (Burt Lancaster) and the professional publicists (personified by Tony Curtis's sleazy Sidney Falco) who feed him material and whose livelihood depends on his beneficence.

(Career note: Many consider *The Sweet Smell of Success* to be Burt Lancaster's finest film, but he has had so many outstanding performances that it's impossible to single one out. Other impressive Lancaster films discussed in this book include *Judgment at Nuremberg, Apache, Gunfight at the OK Corral,* and *Seven Days in May.* Underappreciated for much of his career, his stature is likely to grow considerably over time. For other Lancaster films of interest for family viewing, see Appendix B.)

Journalism's Image Change

The popular image of journalists changed radically after daily newspapers played a major role in Washington's Watergate scandal of the early 1970s. Reporters were suddenly celebrities, tapped into the hot stories and in touch with the world's elite. They basked in the reflected glow of their subjects, and the era of glamour journalism was born.

All the President's Men (1976) is the only film to date that deals directly with these catalytic events, relating the story of *Washington Post* reporters Carl Bernstein and Bob Woodward (Dustin Hoffman and Robert Redford) in breaking the Watergate story. As a primer on the new "attack journalism," the film shows how news sources can be pressured into cooperating with reporters and dramatizes the risks in applying standards of accuracy on fast-breaking stories too loosely. As for the turn to glamour that Watergate represented for the press, look no farther than the credits: you can't do much better than Hoffman and Redford. (For more on *All the President's Men,* see the following discussion of political films.)

Absence of Malice (1981) is a dandy post-Watergate crime versus justice thriller in which an investigative reporter (Sally Field) acts on a U.S. Justice Department tip and helps implicate a suspected organized crime leader (Paul Newman) in some labor union funny business. Along the way, the movie (written by former reporter Kurt Luedtke) becomes a textbook study in newspaper libel law and how reporters deal with news leaks, controversial public figures, and unattributed sources.

The ultimate challenge for any reporter is distinguishing between their roles as observers and participants in the passing drama. The temptation to exploit their unique situation is great, but doing so can result in even greater public calamity. *The Front Page* touches on this issue when Hildy hides escaped convict Earl Williams from the police, in order to scoop competing newspapers by getting Williams' exclusive story.

The participant versus observer theme takes a profound moral twist in Peter Weir's excellent *The Year of Living Dangerously* (1983). Australian radio journalist Guy Hamilton (Mel Gibson), newly arrived in Jakarta during the last years of the Sukarno dictatorship, befriends a native Indonesian photographer (Linda Hunt), who confronts Guy with a central dilemma for journalists in a revolutionary situation: how to remain a neutral observer when you are enveloped in a titanic right versus wrong confrontation, and everyone you come into contact with is taking a side.

In *Under Fire* (1983), the morality issue is raised in a more volatile context and the journalist's participation is carried to an extreme. Here, a free-lance American photojournalist (Nick Nolte) covering the Sandinista revolution in Nicaragua in the late 1970s, knowingly helps the guerrillas spread a fraudulent news story that he knows is designed to advance their struggle against the Somoza government.

(Note to parents: Both *The Year of Living Dangerously* and *Under Fire* are rated R, for scenes of violence and use of profanity. However, both are exceptionally effective in telling their stories, and use the objectionable content in wholly believable context.)

In *Cry Freedom* (1987), South African journalist Donald Woods (Kevin Kline) risks his life and flees his homeland in order to tell the world the story of black South African activist Steven Biko (Denzel Washington). In doing so, Woods/Kline goes well beyond becoming a participant, adapting the role of international advocate for one side in an ongoing social struggle he had originally been assigned to cover as an ostensibly objective journalist.

Politics, Politicians, and the Political Process

Given the great U.S. political dramas of the past two-hundred-plus years, from the Hamilton-Burr shootout to current showdowns between Congress and the president, backstage politics and back-stabbing politicians would appear to be ideal movie subject matter. Not so. Maybe this is true in Europe (where, some would say, every film is political) but not in America. Here, politics has traditionally been a Hollywood taboo, thought by studio executives to be surefire box office poison.

The few overtly political films worth discussing here provide viewers with a perspective that ranges from back room ward bosses to backwoods demagogues, from high-tech television studios to somber Supreme Court chambers. These films are notable because they tell us about American electoral and government processes and the personalities that make them tick. They take us places that otherwise exist only in newspapers and books, providing young viewers with a compelling visual dimension to the flat landscapes of classroom texts (assuming that young viewers are warned that movies are not to be seen as replicating real life).

Looking Inside the Political Process

The local political boss who transforms his electoral turf into a virtual fiefdom is one of the great characters of American political folklore. Two fine movies, both based on real personalities, give us contrasting portraits of the phenomenon at work. *The Last Hurrah* (1958) focuses on the mayor of a northern industrial city, a wily political sophisticate based on Boston's legendary James Michael Curley. *All the King's Men* (1949) concentrates on a rural southern governor, a loutish rustic based on Louisiana's Huey P. Long. Both movies go a long way toward explaining the reality behind the cliche that "all politics is local."

In the big-city variation, the "hurrah" is for Frank Skeffington (Spencer Tracy), the long-time Irish Catholic mayor of a large (unnamed) New England city who is running for reelection for what he says is the last time. Skeffington is presented as the last of a breed: champion of the immigrant poor, tweaker of rich bluenoses, friend to widows, foe of buffoons, and architect of a well-oiled political machine.

Skeffington-style bosses are a political anachronism in the second half of the twentieth century, having been replaced by reform-minded politicians dedicated to more democratic practices (here represented by Skeffington's reporter nephew, played by Jeffrey Hunter). *The Last Hurrah,* adapted from Edwin O'Connor's best-selling novel, is both applauding this political transformation and looking affectionately on one of its last practitioners, as indicated by the casting of the lovable Tracy as Skeffington.

Based on Robert Penn Warren's Pulitzer Prize-winning novel, *All the King's Men* is a rough slap in the face of political naivete. Here we see local politics at its worst—greedy, rapacious, vulgar, and violent. But like Skeffington, the movie's Huey Long stand-in—called Willie Stark (Broderick Crawford)—derives his power not from force or coercion but from a gut-level connection with masses of voters. Stark exploits popular emotions to create a political movement designed to take him all the way to the White House.

Stark fails (just as Long failed), but his failure has nothing to do with political defeat or popular will. The movie underlines the fragility of the political process when it is hit full bore by a powerful, charismatic personal force amply fueled by financial support and abetted by a complacent electorate. *All the Kings Men* won the Academy Award for best picture of 1949, and Broderick Crawford won an Oscar for his portrayal of Stark.

Switching from local politics to the national stage, the Spencer Tracy-Katharine Hepburn comic drama *State of the Union* (1948) is a superior behind-the-scenes look at how presidential tickets were assembled before the age of network television and superstar primaries. This is old-boy power-brokering at its venerable best, reflecting a time when regional bosses could deliver huge blocs of delegate votes and party elders sitting in smoke-filled rooms could shape a national ticket to their liking.

This is an ambitiously prescient film that addresses the weaknesses of the nominating and electoral system, while upholding the virtues of the democratic process. Directed by Frank Capra, it can be seen as an extension of his earlier film *Mr. Smith Goes to Washington* (see description later in this section), with its combination of satire, drama, and do-gooder handwringing.

In *State of the Union,* Tracy plays Grant Matthews, a high-minded Republican businessman and dark-horse presidential candidate who tries to rise above the process (not unlike the GOP's dark-horse, nonpolitician candidate Dwight Eisenhower in 1952). Once his candidacy begins to take off, Matthews is torn between a temptation to tailor his outspoken opinions to fit the popular mood and the need to maintain his integrity, doing the right thing by his friends, family, party, and country.

A more jaundiced view of the political nominating process and the party bosses who controlled it is found in *The Best Man* (1964), the film version of a successful Gore Vidal play. Here the virtuous presidential candidate is a bookish liberal secretary of state (Henry Fonda) who refuses to use some scandalous material against his chief rival, a demagogic conservative U.S. senator (Cliff Robertson), even though the senator is threatening to use smear tactics against the secretary. Vidal's script successfully dramatizes a key personal issue for politicians that has figured in national politics as recently as the 1992 presidential primaries: the need to appear as a strong, forceful leader versus the need to maintain a conscience-driven sense of decency without making ruinous compromises or engaging, as Vidal would have it, in "small corruptions."

Beginning in the late 1960s, the real-world campaign role of back-room power brokers and regional bosses was largely supplanted by free-lance political consultants and media advisers. In movie terms, they were a variation on a familiar Hollywood type: lone gunslingers selling their services to the highest bidder and then riding off into the sunset when the dust had settled after the high-noon electoral showdown. No candidate is known to have hollered "Come back, Shane" after a departing consultant, but many have no doubt felt like doing so.

A superb look at this not altogether happy development is provided in *The Candidate* (1972), a Robert Redford vehicle that is so definitive in its insights into modern politics that it is frequently given textbookish references in reporters' campaign coverage. In *The Candidate,* consultant-for-hire Marvin Lucas (Peter Boyle) swoops into California, seeks out the liberal Democrat son of an ex-governor (Redford), and persuades the political newcomer to run for the U.S. Senate against a popular Republican incumbent. Redford's character agrees to run, is placed in the hands of a savvy media guru, and pulls off a stunning upset victory. The negative side of the new breed of candidate and campaign depicted here is reflected in the movie's final line, when victorious candidate Redford turns to his campaign guru moments after the election and asks, "Hey, Marvin, what do we do now?"

While *The Candidate* focuses on a Senate campaign, the phenomenon it highlights has been found in several subsequent national campaigns with an unsettling image-over-substance tone: the presidential campaigns of Jimmy Carter in 1976, Ronald Reagan and Gary Hart in 1984, and George Bush and Michael Dukakis in 1988. Its most impressive foreshadowing, however, was the 1974 California gubernatorial election, when Jerry Brown, liberal Democrat son of a former governor and political newcomer, won an upset victory.

Taking Us Inside Washington

The ultimate goal of every red-blooded American politician is to hold federal office in Washington, D.C. In moviemaking, however, the workings of the federal government have been no more popular a subject than politics and the political process, and understandably so. Until the 1960s, the nation's capital was a sleepy backwater burg with the general cosmopolitan ambience of a prairie crossroads, where the streets emptied early in the evening and the whole city emptied in the summer.

Now Washington is an exciting, vibrant international city, and the episode that helped to transform the capital's dynamic also resulted in one of the best recent films about the city's socio-political infrastructure: the break-in of Democratic National Headquarters at the Watergate Office Building in 1972, the subsequent White House cover-up, and the eventual forced resignation of President Richard Nixon in 1974.

The film that captures many of these events (and the events behind the events), *All the President's Men* (1976), dwells on a side of official Washington not found in civics texts, a venue where reporters doggedly pursue wisps of scandal and middle-level functionaries serve as eager sources, their motives ranging from mean vindictiveness to selfless idealism. Both *All the President's Men* and the scandal on which it is based changed Washington and how it works. Politically, Watergate sparked an era of ethical puritanism that has since toppled numerous office holders and candidates. For members of the working press, the *Washington Post* expose of the scandal, by reporters Bob Woodward and Carl Bernstein (and their on-screen depiction by superstars Robert Redford and Dustin Hoffman, respectively), gave an unassailable glamour to Washington journalism and, with it, a lusting drive for the fame that comes to those who bag the mighty.

As moviemaking, *All the President's Men* performs the formidable cinematic trick of treating an important subject with intelligence and respect and still producing a heart-pounding, slam-bang action-adventure picture. It's an excellent movie to watch with children, and requires only a bit of historical background to set up the plot.

In the capital's more familiar official precincts, all three branches of constitutional government have provided the setting for recommended motion pictures. Casting its lenses at the congressional branch sitting on Capitol Hill, Hollywood has given us Frank Capra's aforementioned *Mr. Smith Goes to Washington* (1939), the sentimental, lighthearted story of an idealistic young senator's effort to thwart a legislative land grab, and *Advise and Consent* (1962), a windy but watchable study of congressional politics that is still as fresh as tomorrow's headlines.

In the first of these movies, James Stewart's Jefferson Smith is the homespun leader of a midwestern state boys' club who, on gubernatorial whim, is appointed to a vacant Senate seat. Barely settled in, Smith takes up the issue of establishing a national boys' camp on land that turns out to be targeted for a lucrative development project by his home-state political mentors. Under the tutelage of a sassy, street-smart political aide (Jean Arthur), Smith undertakes a highly cinematic Senate filibuster and wins the legislative battle, as well as his aide's affections.

While it may be difficult to imagine Smith's cause attracting much more than passing attention in contemporary Washington, his character presents a model of integrity and rectitude that time should not diminish. In Jefferson Smith (and *State of the Union*'s Grant Matthews), director Capra is merely doing what drama has been doing since ancient Greece: holding out an ideal model of behavior that ordinary people may not achieve but to which they should aspire.

Less idealistic than Capra's Mr. Smith, Otto Preminger's *Advise and Consent* centers on the Senate confirmation battle over the president's appointment of a liberal pacifist (Henry Fonda) to the post of secretary of state and the attendant intrigue that surrounds the confirmation process. Based on a novel by longtime Washington journalist Allen Drury, *Advise and Consent* has a gritty insider feel to its deliberate detailing of Senate customs and practices, with the plot twists including allegations of pro-Communist sympathies, homosexual practices, and presidential incompetence.

(Career note: Henry Fonda's presence in three of the films listed in this section confirms his status as the Hollywood actor most successful at presenting national movie audiences with their most reassuring image of their leaders. Fonda was stern, sensitive, virtuous bedrock American stock at its best, and we were willing to follow him anywhere, through almost fifty years of moviemaking. Late in his career, Fonda decided that he would like, for once, to play a villain and did so superbly in *Once Upon a Time in the West.* For other Fonda films of interest for family viewing, see Appendix B.)

Meanwhile, down Pennsylvania Avenue at the White House, *Seven Days in May* (1964) pits a controversial liberal president (Fredric March) in desperate battle with a band of renegade right-wing military officers over the issue of a pending disarmament treaty. This is first-class drama, presenting serious issues with entertaining polish and a reassuring backstage authenticity. It is notable that in this movie's plot bristling with suspense, intrigue, and conspiracy, there is not a single scene of violence or a single gunshot.

Seven Days in May is also an excellent film to watch with children in the context of renewed interest in the assassination of President John F. Kennedy in 1963. As the movie was in production at the time of the assassination, and as it involved a frighteningly bitter dispute between the military and the President, it provides keen insight into the sharply confrontational national politics of that time.

Disarmament issues were among the most controversial political agenda items of the period, and two other respected films share this subject, as well as a White House focus, with *Seven Days in May. Fail-Safe* (1964) is a gloomy depiction of a solitary president (Fonda again) facing the trade-offs involved in potential global destruction. *Dr. Strangelove, Or: How I Learned to Stop Worrying and Love the Bomb* (1964) is one of the most gloriously wicked satires ever filmed, featuring a President (Peter Sellers) who is a virtual – and unintentional – parody of the characters depicted by Fonda and March in the other two films.

Dr. Strangelove is an especially good film for viewing with children, as they will appreciate the broad humor of Sellers (who plays three roles in the picture), George C. Scott as General Buck Turgidson, and Slim Pickens as the captain of the unthinkingly persistent bomber crew that manages to penetrate Russian airspace. Adults will enjoy all this, too, as well as the subtle political satire, including the Kissinger-like character of presidential adviser Strangelove.

Finally, for a behind-the-scenes look at the judicial branch, we have *First Monday in October* (1981), a discursive, well-meaning film that pits a new female conservative Supreme Court justice (Jill Clayburgh) against her most liberal male colleague (Walter Matthau) – a novel plot twist that was overtaken by the real-life appointment of conservative justice Sandra Day O'Connor shortly after the movie's release. (The gentleman liberal is loosely based on former Justice William O. Douglas.)

First Monday in October is notable for its rare and informative look inside the Supreme Court and the genial good humor with which it approaches the judicial issue on which the plot hinges – First Amendment rights in obscenity cases. The movie shows backstage court life as a lively and considerate give-and-take intellectual exercise to investigate judicial issues, examine constitutional nuances, and build a court consensus. This may not be daily reality, but it does give young viewers a peek inside the high court.

(Note to parents: Because part of the plot in *First Monday in October* involves the free-speech rights of a movie theater to show pornographic films, the movie is rated R. However, the objectionable material is limited to a brief snippet from the film in question and attendant profanity. Otherwise, *First Monday in October* contains no overtly objectionable material and is a valuable primer on Supreme Court proceedings.)

For an excellent cinematic recreation of the process involved in preparing a landmark case for presentation before the Supreme Court, see the discussion of *Separate But Equal* (1991) in the section on movies focusing on racial relations. This fine, made-for-TV drama, starring Burt Lancaster and Sidney Poitier, concerns a monumental school desegregation case decided by the Supreme Court in the early 1950s. Poitier plays Thurgood Marshall, the NAACP legal counsel who was appointed as an associate justice to the Supreme Court in the 1960s.

Chapter 6

Quick Reference
Movie Reviews

Each of the movies listed here is discussed in one of the themed sections in chapter 5, and is cross-referenced to the theme discussions for your convenience. We have included these capsule reviews for those readers who find it helpful to scan a list before heading out to rent a video or two.

■ **Abe Lincoln in Illinois.** Raymond Massey, Gene Lockhart, Ruth Gordon, Howard da Silva. 1940, B&W, 110 minutes. A series of vignettes traces Lincoln's life from his log-cabin boyhood through his election to the presidency and departure from Springfield, Illinois, to Washington. The combination of highly realistic design, grandly literate script (based on a Pulitzer Prize-winning play), and Massey's for-the-ages portrayal of Lincoln makes this the best of the few presidential screen bios. Exquisite combination of entertainment and education. Not rated. Recommended for all ages. (See page 58.)

■ **Absence of Malice.** Paul Newman, Sally Field, Melinda Dillon, Wilford Brimley, Bob Balaban. 1981, color, 116 minutes. Reporter Field deals with manipulative government officials and confronts profound ethical issues while attempting to pursue a story on reputed organized crime figure Newman. The tough script (written by a former newsman) offers a sobering perspective on post-Watergate "attack journalism," with the added plus of a plausible, intricate plot and predictably appealing performances by the two stars. Rated PG. Most appreciated by ages ten and over. (See page 106.)

■ **Adam's Rib.** Spencer Tracy, Katharine Hepburn, Judy Holliday, Tom Ewell, David Wayne. 1949, B&W/colorized, 100 minutes. Tracy and Hepburn play husband-and-wife lawyers who suddenly find they're opposing each other in a courtroom case involving a woman accused of a crime-of-passion murder. One of the best Tracy-Hepburn comedies, it is smart, funny, and offers a prescient commentary on women's rights. Comedienne Holliday is unforgettable as the not-so-dumb blonde, accused murderer. Not rated. Recommended for all ages. (See page 90.)

■ **Advise and Consent.** Henry Fonda, Don Murray, Charles Laughton, Franchot Tone, Lew Ayres, Peter Lawford, Gene Tierney, Burgess Meredith, Paul Ford. 1962, B&W, 139 minutes. Contentious Senate battle over the nomination of liberal pacifist Fonda to be secretary of state is the backdrop for a look at the inner workings of Capitol Hill. Based on the best-selling novel by longtime Washington correspondent Allen Drury. Astute political observers will relish the casting of Kennedy in-law Lawford as a skirt-chasing New England Senator (the film was released during the Kennedy administration). And watch for Betty White, of television's "The Mary Tyler Moore Show" and "Golden Girls," as a senator from Kansas. Not rated. Most appreciated by ages twelve and over. (See page 111.)

■ **All About Eve.** Bette Davis, Anne Baxter, George Sanders, Celeste Holm, Gary Merrill, Thelma Ritter, Marilyn Monroe. 1950, B&W, 138 minutes. Definitive backstage look at Broadway theater world, as aspiring actress Baxter cynically exploits her friendship with over-the-hill star Davis. Davis's grand performance, superlative supporting cast (including Monroe in a showstopping bit part), and exemplary script give the drama uncommon vitality and veracity. Oscars: Best picture, director (Joseph L. Mankiewicz), supporting actor (Sanders). Not rated. Most appreciated by ages fourteen and over. (See page 77.)

■ **All the King's Men.** Broderick Crawford, Mercedes McCambridge, John Ireland, John Derek. 1949, B&W, 109 minutes. Spectacular rise and astonishing fall of a dangerous backwoods southern demagogue who, after being elected governor, casts his eye on the White House and national power. Based on the Pulitzer Prize-winning novel by Robert Penn Warren, which was itself loosely based on Louisiana governor and U.S. senator Huey P. Long. Oscars: Best picture, actor (Crawford), supporting actress (McCambridge). Not rated. Most appreciated by ages twelve and over. (See page 108.)

■ **All the President's Men.** Dustin Hoffman, Robert Redford, Jason Robards, Martin Balsam, Hal Holbrook, Jane Alexander, Ned Beatty. 1976, color, 138 minutes. Industrious journalism that uncovered the shocking Watergate scandal and led to the 1974 resignation of President Richard Nixon is recast in the mode of an edge-of-your-seat suspense thriller. Jam-packed with insights into official Washington and big-city media, with many characters and scenes that seem plucked from daily capital life. Oscar: Best supporting actor (Robards). Rated PG. Most appreciated by ages twelve and over. (See page 106.)

■ **Anatomy of a Murder.** James Stewart, Lee Remick, George C. Scott, Ben Gazzara, Arthur O'Connell, Eve Arden. 1959, B&W, 160 minutes. Folksy, small-town lawyer Stewart does battle with slick, big-city prosecutor Scott (in one of his first screen roles) in the case of a GI accused of killing the man who assaulted his wife. Courtroom drama at its best, aided by another great Stewart performance and the crackling energy of young Scott. Arden, of Television's "Our Miss Brooks," plays Stewart's office manager. Not rated, but the case does involve rape and attendant sexual matters. Most appreciated by ages twelve and over. (See page 90.)

■ **Andromeda Strain, The.** Arthur Hill, David Wayne, Kate Reid, James Olson. 1971, color, 130 minutes. Scientists race to determine the nature of a mysterious otherworldly virus before it infects all humankind. Scientific thriller manages to squeeze excitement and tension from a story where most of the action happens under a lab microscope. Rated G. Most appreciated by ages eight and over. (See page 86.)

■ **Angels with Dirty Faces.** James Cagney, Pat O'Brien, Humphrey Bogart, Ann Sheridan, George Bancroft. 1938, B&W/colorized, 97 minutes. Streetwise Cagney grows from juvenile delinquent to big-time hoodlum, idolized by a new generation of New York City slum punks. Meanwhile, Cagney's boyhood pal O'Brien, now a priest, begs him to help steer his young fans away from crime. The best of the 1930s gangster pictures for mixing human-interest melodrama, humor, and romance with crime action. Surefire entertainment for young audiences, and its message still packs a wallop. Not rated. Recommended for all ages. (See page 42.)

■ **Apache.** Burt Lancaster, Jean Peters, Charles Bronson. 1954, color, 91 minutes. A young Apache Indian (Lancaster) refuses to go quietly with his people to a new reservation. He flees and launches a one-man rebellion against the seizure of former tribal lands in the Southwest. Early sympathetic depiction of Native American mistreatment, albeit with white actors (in typical Hollywood tradition) playing Indian roles. Not rated. Recommended for all ages. (See page 73.)

■ **Awful Truth, The.** Cary Grant, Irene Dunne, Ralph Bellamy. 1937, B&W, 92 minutes. Grant and Dunne are divorced but so ideally matched that they dedicate themselves to making each other humorously miserable. When you hear the phrase "screwball comedy," this is what it means. Never out of date and never funnier than right now. Oscar: Best director, Leo McCarey. Not rated. Recommended for all ages. (See page 37.)

■ **Bad and the Beautiful, The.** Kirk Douglas, Lana Turner, Dick Powell, Gloria Grahame, Barry Sullivan, Walter Pidgeon, Gilbert Roland. 1952, B&W/colorized, 118 minutes. Movie producer Douglas, unable to raise money for his first film in two years, turns to three friends – a top director, a writer, and an actress – to help him stage a comeback. The three then describe their careers in flashback, providing lively, caustic commentary on the movie business. Not rated. Most appreciated by ages fourteen and over. (See page 79.)

■ **Bananas.** Woody Allen, Louise Lasser, Howard Cosell. 1971, color, 82 minutes. Jilted by his political activist girlfriend Lasser, Allen flees to a fictitious Latin American nation to fight a revolution, becoming the nation's president when the rebels are victorious. Vintage Allen zaniness – a four-star combination of satire and slapstick – takes a swipe at television, politics, psychiatrists, lawyers, and more. Allen ordering a take-out lunch for his entire rebel army is a favorite bit. That's Sylvester Stallone playing one of the subway thugs early in the picture. Rated PG. Recommended for all ages. (See page 41.)

■ **Best Man, The.** Henry Fonda, Cliff Robertson, Shelley Berman, Ann Southern, Edie Adams. 1964, B&W, 102 minutes. Backstage wrangling over a presidential nomination at the national party convention pits nice-guy liberal Fonda against right-wing guttersnipe Robertson. This high-minded political soap opera, written by Gore Vidal, provides an interesting perspective on the modern presidential nominating process. Not rated. Most appreciated by ages fourteen and over. (See page 109.)

■ **Blackboard Jungle, The.** Glenn Ford, Sidney Poitier, Anne Francis, Vic Morrow, Richard Kiley. 1955, B&W, 101 minutes. New teacher Ford is given a memorably rough time by teenage toughs at a New York City all-boys vocational school with a notorious discipline problem. This seminal 1950s juvenile delinquent picture shocked the nation with its grim take on urban youth crime and its disturbing implication of things to come. First "youth movie" to understand the pivotal cultural role of rock and roll, then in its infancy, by grafting "Rock Around the Clock" onto the otherwise all-jazz sound track. Poitier's breakthrough movie and the film debut of Morrow, later the star of television's "Combat." Not rated. Most appreciated by ages ten and over. (See page 44.)

■ **Blob, The.** Steve McQueen, Aneta Corseaut. 1958, color, 86 minutes. Gloppy object from outer space threatens to engulf an entire town in its gelatinous mass until some clever townies discover its weak spot. One of the first plucky-teens-against-alien-enemies sci-fi pictures and the first starring role for young "Steven" McQueen. Not rated. Recommended for all ages. (See page 50.)

■ **Bound for Glory.** David Carradine, Ronny Cox, Melinda Dillon, Randy Quaid. 1976, color, 147 minutes. Before achieving national fame as a pioneering folk troubadour, Woody Guthrie (Carradine) suffers the poverty, separation from his family, and political persecution that were to fuel his songwriting and singing talents. Vibrant biography of a major, underappreciated American musical artist.

Many fine Guthrie tunes on the sound track. Rated PG. Recommended for all ages. (See page 95.)

■ **Boys Town.** Spencer Tracy, Mickey Rooney, Henry Hull. 1938, B&W, 96 minutes. Based on true-life story of Father Edward Flanagan, a Roman Catholic priest in Omaha, Nebraska, who persuades city fathers to finance his idealistic dream of establishing a rural residence for wayward boys who might otherwise turn to a life of crime. The movie's central drama focuses on the test of wills between the good Father and one of his earliest recruits, tough street kid Rooney who thumbs his nose at the goodie-goodie Boys Town culture. Oscar: Best actor (Tracy). Not rated. Most appreciated by ages ten and over. (See page 43.)

■ **Breaking Away.** Dennis Christopher, Dennis Quaid, Daniel Stern, Jackie Earle Haley, Hart Bochner, Amy Wright, Barbara Barrie. 1979, color, 100 minutes. Just out of high school and with nothing to do, four midwestern youths decide to take on the stuck-up local college boys in a five-hundred lap bicycle race. Even though it was nominated for a best picture Oscar, this film is considered a sleeper treasure by its devoted cult fans. A fresh, original work of gentle charm, wit, and insight – a real winner. Rated PG. Recommended for all ages. (See page 104.)

■ **Bride of Frankenstein, The.** Boris Karloff, Elsa Lanchester, Colin Clive, Valerie Hobson, John Carradine. 1935, B&W, 75 minutes. Dr. Frankenstein's monster did not die in the windmill fire after all but lives on in this sequel, acquiring man-made "bride" Lanchester and getting loose in the English countryside. One of the most successful sequels ever made, this witty, wonderfully performed classic contains many of the scenes usually associated with *Frankenstein* (the blind hermit, for example). Not rated. Recommended for all ages. (See page 47.)

■ **Broadway Danny Rose.** Woody Allen, Mia Farrow, Nick Apollo Forte. 1984, color, 86 minutes. Hustling New York talent agent Danny Rose (Allen), forever scratching out a living on the fringes of show business, finally finds a potential gold mine in lounge singer Forte, who promptly complicates the situation by falling for Mafia moll Farrow. Detail-rich comedy on the lovable, sometimes pathetic underside of show biz. Rated PG. Most appreciated by ages twelve and over. (See page 76.)

■ **Buddy Holly Story, The.** Gary Busey, Charles Martin Smith, Don Stroud, Maria Richwine. 1978, color, 113 minutes. A major force in bringing black rhythm and blues into the rock mainstream, Holly (Busey) is seen leaving his Lubbock, Texas, home and achieving overnight national success with his band, The Crickets, and songs such as "Peggy Sue." Purists say the movie distorts the real Holly story, but it remains the most entertaining rock biopic as much for Busey's performance as for Holly's vitality and creativity. Rated PG. Recommended for all ages. (See page 96.)

■ **Burn!** Marlon Brando. 1969, color, 112 minutes. British adventurer William Walker (Brando) stirs up a native revolt that will ultimately help his corporate employer by replacing an unfriendly government with a friendly one. Colorful real-life rebel Walker presented in a vivid, offbeat political adventure tale (somewhat retold in the violent, sordid 1988 movie, *Walker,* which is not recommended). Rated PG. Most appreciated by ages ten and over. (See page 56.)

■ **Caine Mutiny, The.** Humphrey Bogart, Jose Ferrer, Fred MacMurray, Van Johnson, E. G. Marshall, Robert Francis, Lee Marvin. 1954, color, 125 minutes. Officers of the USS *Caine* seize command of the ship from Captain Philip Francis Queeg (Bogart) and must justify their mutinous actions before a Navy court martial by painting Queeg as a tyrannical, eccentric incompetent. Exceptional use of military proceeding as setting for courtroom drama, and the final judgment is in question to the end. Originally a Herman Wouk novel and Broadway play. Not rated. Most appreciated by ages eight and over. (See page 91.)

■ **Candidate, The.** Robert Redford, Peter Boyle, Melvyn Douglas. 1972, color, 109 minutes. Political gun-for-hire Boyle persuades campaign novice Redford to challenge a popular incumbent U.S. senator. Redford wins through clever use of the media and image manipulation, and then asks mentor Boyle, "What do we do now?" Anticipates the 1974 California gubernatorial election of Jerry Brown and numerous image-driven presidential campaigns. A highly regarded look at modern campaign management. Rated PG, with modest sexual situations. Most appreciated by ages fourteen and over. (See page 110.)

■ **Captains Courageous.** Spencer Tracy, Freddie Bartholomew, Lionel Barrymore, Melvyn Douglas, John Carradine, Mickey Rooney. 1937, B&W/colorized, 116 minutes. Spoiled rich kid Bartholomew gets a taste of real life when he tumbles off an ocean liner and is rescued by a crew of working-class fishermen manning a boat out of Gloucester. Heartwarming action movie (based on Rudyard Kipling novel) details an earnestly believable coming-of-age experience. Remarkable shipboard effects, given that the movie was filmed in a studio tank. Oscar: Best actor (Tracy). Not rated. Recommended for all ages. (See page 99.)

■ **Casablanca.** Humphrey Bogart, Ingrid Bergman, Claude Rains, Paul Henreid, Peter Lorre, Sidney Greenstreet, Dooley Wilson. 1942, B&W/colorized, 102 minutes. Ilsa Lund (Bergman) comes to Rick's Cafe in Casablanca with her Resistance hero husband (Henreid), last stop on their flight to America, and rekindles her love for proprietor Rick Blaine (Bogart). For adults, it's a wonderful grown-up romance. For kids, it's Nazis, spies, and underground fighters. For everyone, it's probably the greatest American movie ever made. You can't see it too many times. Oscars: Best picture, director (Michael Curtiz). Not rated. Recommended for all ages. (See page 83.)

■ **Charly.** Cliff Robertson, Claire Bloom, Lilia Skala, Dick Van Patten. 1968, color, 103 minutes. Mentally retarded Charlie (he spells it "Charly") Gordon (Robertson) is subjected to a medical experiment that feeds his brain intense doses of protein, dramatically enhancing his mental ability to a near-genius level. Along the way, he wins the heart of his spunky teacher (Bloom). Earnest drama of the social traumas of mentally-challenged persons, told with a dollop of sci-fi gimmickry. Oscar: Best actor (Robertson). Rated PG. Most appreciated by ages twelve and over. (See page 60.)

■ **Cheyenne Autumn.** Richard Widmark, Carroll Baker, Karl Malden, Sal Mineo, Edward G. Robinson, James Stewart, Arthur Kennedy, Ricardo Montalban, Gilbert Roland. 1964, color, 145 minutes. Destitute Cheyenne tribe undertakes arduous trek from its bleak Oklahoma reservation dumping ground back to the fertile Wyoming lands it was driven from. Based on historic events, John Ford's last Western is a moving tribute to the spirit and culture of Native Americans, whom his earlier films often depicted in a less flattering light. Not rated. Most appreciated by ages ten and over. (See page 73.)

■ **China Syndrome, The.** Jack Lemmon, Jane Fonda, Michael Douglas, Wilford Brimley. 1979, color, 123 minutes. Aggressive TV reporter Fonda and cameraman Douglas investigate a scandal at a nuclear power facility, aided by rebellious plant executive Lemmon and frustrated by plant management and their own newsroom superiors. Powerful antinuke message wrapped up in an exciting meltdown melodrama. Rated PG. Most appreciated by ages ten and over. (See page 87.)

■ **Chorus Line, A.** Michael Douglas, Vicki Frederick, Janet Jones, Audrey Landers. 1985, color, 113 minutes. A group of aspiring singer-dancers try out for a new musical, and in the elimination process, much is learned about their personalities and psyches and what it takes to make it on Broadway. Douglas presides as the show's director. Based on the longest-running musical in Broadway history. Maybe not the same as seeing it live onstage, but still a memorable experience that is intensely personal and creatively exhilarating. Rated PG (some of the personal confessions are very personal). Most appreciated by ages twelve and over. (See page 77.)

■ **Children of a Lesser God.** William Hurt, Marlee Matlin, Piper Laurie, Philip Bosco. 1986, color, 110 minutes. Speech teacher Hurt begins new job at a school

for the deaf and embarks on a sometimes rocky relationship with school gradu-
ate (now custodian) Matlin. The primary point of contention between the pair is
her insistence on communicating by signing and his on teaching her to speak.
Outstanding presentation of the lives and inner turmoil of deaf youngsters, told in
the context of a very modern love story. Oscar: Best actress (Matlin). Rated R for
infrequent profanity and sexual content. Most appreciated by ages fourteen and
over. (See page 64.)

■ **Citizen Kane.** Orson Welles, Joseph Cotten, Everett Sloane, Agnes Moorehead,
Dorothy Comingore. 1941, B&W, 119 minutes. Story of Charles Foster Kane
(said to be modeled on publishing magnate William Randolph Hearst) told in
flashbacks after the tycoon dies with the elliptical utterance "rosebud" on his lips.
Thought by many critics to be the best-made movie ever, *Kane* was the first
feature directed by boy wonder Welles (who also plays Kane). Vivid depiction of
the unbridled political, social, and cultural power enjoyed by the early American
press barons. Not rated. Most appreciated by ages fourteen and over. (See page
105.)

■ **Close Encounters of the Third Kind.** Richard Dreyfuss, Teri Garr, Francois
Truffaut, Melinda Dillon, Cary Guffey. 1977, color, 135 minutes. Midwest tele-
phone lineman Dreyfuss has a UFO sighting that leads him, along with dozens of
other "close-encounter" witnesses, to a significant Wyoming mountaintop meeting between extraterrestrials and earthlings. The first "important" movie to treat
UFOs seriously and depict "aliens" as benign visitors. Thrilling entertainment
whatever the viewer thinks about intelligent life elsewhere in the universe. Rated
PG. Recommended for all ages (some scenes may frighten younger children).
(See page 51.)

■ **Coal Miner's Daughter.** Sissy Spacek, Tommy Lee Jones, Beverly D'Angelo.
1980, color, 125 minutes. Colorful, pungent screen biography follows country
singer Loretta Lynn from an impoverished Appalachian childhood to Grand Ol'
Opry glory in an inspiring, emotional rags-to-riches story. It is a convincing
behind-the-scenes look at country music stardom. Spacek stars and sings her
own songs in a virtuoso Oscar-winning performance. Rated PG for brief sexual
dialogue and one modest bedroom scene. Recommended for all ages. (See
page 95.)

■ **Coma.** Michael Douglas, Genevieve Bujold, Elizabeth Ashley, Rip Torn, Richard
Widmark. 1978, color, 113 minutes. Gutsy young medic Bujold tries to persuade
her surgeon boyfriend Douglas to help her investigate mysterious deaths at the
hospital where they work. Top-notch medical thriller (from novelist Robin Cook's
first best-seller), inspired by increased traffic in human organ donations for
transplants. Television's "Magnum P.I." (Tom Selleck) debuts on film as a patient.

Rated PG (some of the corpses are briefly glimpsed unclothed). Most appreciated by ages ten and over. (See page 86.)

■ **Cowboys, The.** John Wayne, Roscoe Lee Browne, Bruce Dern, Coleen Dewhurst, Slim Pickens, Robert Carradine, A. Martinez. 1972, color, 128 minutes. Montana rancher Wayne recruits eleven schoolboys to help him drive his cattle herd 400 miles to market, after his cowhands all run off to pan for gold. Rites-of-passage film records the boys' maturation as they deal with the ordeals of the trail, including a gang of ruffians intent on stealing the herd. Notable performances by theater stars Dewhurst as Wayne's wife and Browne as the trail cook. Outstanding John Williams score. Rated PG for occasional violence. Most appreciated by ages twelve and over. (See page 100.)

■ **Cry Freedom.** Denzel Washington, Kevin Kline, Zakes Mokae, Alec McCowen. 1987, color, 157 minutes. Heroic story of black South African activist Steven Biko (Washington), his death in police custody, and the efforts of white journalist Donald Woods (Kline) to tell Biko's story. This lengthy, faithfully detailed account of true events was criticized for its overemphasis on Woods, who was forced to abandon his family and flee South Africa because of his activities. Still, a rare, sensitive look at the racial tinderbox of South Africa. Rated PG for infrequent, moderate violence. Most appreciated by ages twelve and over. (See page 107.)

■ **Dances with Wolves.** Kevin Costner, Mary McDonnell, Graham Greene. 1990, color, 181 minutes. Following service in the Civil War, Lieutenant John Dunbar (Costner) requests assignment to a frontier outpost, is adopted by a peaceable Sioux tribe, falls in love with a white woman (McDonnell) raised by them, and eases into their life-style. Highly praised and widely honored film — the first Western to win an Oscar in sixty years — most notable for its sympathetic and sensitive treatment of Native American culture. Oscars: Best picture, director (Costner). Rated PG. Recommended for all ages. (See page 72.)

■ **Day for Night.** Francois Truffaut, Jacqueline Bisset, Jean-Pierre Aumont, Valentina Cortese, Jean-Pierre Leaud. 1973, color, 120 minutes. Director/star Truffaut plays a film director very much like himself, dealing with an endless stream of ego problems and assorted crises — many very comical — on the set of a romantic melodrama. Excellent behind-the-scenes perspective on modern international moviemaking. Rated PG. Most appreciated by ages twelve and over. (See page 80.)

■ **Day the Earth Stood Still, The.** Michael Rennie, Patricia Neal, Billy Gray. 1951, B&W, 92 minutes. Friendly alien Klaatu (Rennie) comes to warn earthlings against the careless use of atomic energy and finds himself under attack by suspicious natives, except for a trusting young boy (Gray). Pleasantly accessible and serious-minded sci-fi parable, with enough confrontations and suspense to keep the plot moving. Young Gray was later male sibling Bud on the long-running television hit, "Father Knows Best." Not rated. Recommended for all ages. (See page 50.)

■ **Dead Poets Society.** Robin Williams, Robert Sean Leonard, Ethan Hawke. 1989, color, 128 minutes. New teacher Williams inspires his private-school English class to "gather ye rosebuds while ye may . . . make your lives extraordinary," and several respond by resurrecting – with ultimately tragic results – a hedonist society that Williams himself had launched while a student. Fine story of youth's first awakening to the glories of intellectual creativity and the possibilities of life, with a jolly, powerful performance by Williams. Rated PG for isolated incident of violence, occasional oblique sexual dialogue. Most appreciated by ages ten and over. (See page 101.)

■ **Defiant Ones, The.** Tony Curtis, Sidney Poitier, Theodore Bikel, Lon Chaney, Jr. 1958, B&W, 97 minutes. Two convicts escape from a prison road gang, chained together, and have to act in sync to elude capture. Strong statement for interracial accommodation and harmony made early in the civil rights movement. Director Stanley Kramer later did the even more provocative *Guess Who's Coming to Dinner* (also with Poitier). Stands up well as social commentary and action-adventure picture. Not rated. Most appreciated by ages eight and over. (See page 52.)

■ **Dr. Strangelove; Or, How I Learned to Stop Worrying and Love the Bomb.** Peter Sellers, George C. Scott, Slim Pickens, Sterling Hayden, Keenan Wynn, James Earl Jones. 1964, B&W, 93 minutes. Crazed U.S. Air Force officer Hayden conspires to launch bomber attacks on targets in the USSR, to the consternation of the pacifist U.S. president (Sellers, in one of his three roles) and ill-disguised glee of the U.S. military high command. Elegant sociopolitical satire, but with plenty of action and broad humor to amuse younger viewers. Stanley Kubrick's dark classic warrants, and rewards, repeat viewings. Sellers's performance (including the role of Kissinger-inspired Strangelove himself) is sheer genius. Not rated. Recommended for all ages. (See page 112.)

■ **Dracula.** Bela Lugosi, David Manners, Helen Chandler. 1931, B&W, 75 minutes. Everyone's favorite Transylvanian count leaves his musty, bat-ridden castle and moves to England, which is not good news for certain Londoners. Packed with tasty lore about vampires (or the "undead," as they prefer) and vampirism. Lugosi is a master of elegant menace. Not rated. Recommended for all ages. (See page 47.)

■ **Duck Soup.** Groucho, Chico, Harpo, and Zeppo Marx; Margaret Dumont; Louis Calhern. 1933, B&W, 70 minutes. Rufus T. Firefly (Groucho) becomes prime minister of plucky little Freedonia. The rest is history. Best of the Marx Brothers comedies. Not rated. Recommended for all ages. (See page 36.)

■ **Elvis.** Kurt Russell, Shelley Winters, Pat Hingle, Ed Begley, Jr., Joe Mantegna. 1979, color, 150 minutes. The King struggles through an impoverished Mississippi boyhood, moves to Memphis, and becomes a rock-and-roll legend. Remarkably good rock biopic given the familiarity of the larger-than-life subject. A sensibly unsentimental script and a solid performance by Russell in the title role (country artist Ronnie McDowell covers Elvis's tunes). When originally aired as a made-for-TV movie opposite the first television broadcast of *Gone with the Wind,* *Elvis* grabbed the largest rating of any network television program ever. Not rated. Recommended for all ages. (See page 96.)

■ **Emerald Forest, The.** Powers Boothe, Charlie Boorman, Meg Foster. 1985, color, 113 minutes. American civil engineer Boothe, working on a massive dam project in the Brazilian rain forest, sees his young son kidnapped by a native tribe and spends ten years trying to find him. Powerful message about family bonding and environmental destruction marred by a cold-fish lead character and trite shoot-'em-up climax. Director John Boorman's son Charlie plays the kidnapped Tommy. Rated R for frequent native nudity, infrequent profanity, and moderate violence. Most appreciated by ages twelve and over. (See page 99.)

■ **Empire of the Sun.** Christian Bale, John Malkovich, Miranda Richardson, Nigel Havers. 1987, color, 152 minutes. A British boy, separated from his parents during the evacuation of Shanghai at the start of World War II, grows to maturity while imprisoned in a Japanese POW camp for European and American nationals. Directed by Steven Spielberg, and again showing his uncanny knack for evoking the drama and wonderment of childhood experience. Bale's performance is a knockout. Rated PG for minimal profanity and violence. Most appreciated by ages ten and over. (See page 103.)

■ **E.T. – The Extra-Terrestrial.** Henry Thomas, Dee Wallace, Peter Coyote, Drew Barrymore. 1982, color, 115 minutes. Director Steven Spielberg continues his "alien revisionism," begun with *Close Encounters of the Third Kind,* proposing that creatures from outer space may be benign visitors and not destructive invaders. Here he also makes a strong statement about fear, suspicion, and acceptance of "outsiders" in general. A whimsical sci-fi story about a young boy (Thomas) befriending a gentle extraterrestrial (voice by Debra Winger) left behind by his spaceship. The movie works amazingly well on all levels, becoming that genuine entertainment rarity – a treat for all ages. Rated PG. Recommended for all ages. (See page 51.)

■ **Face in the Crowd, A.** Andy Griffith, Patricia Neal, Walter Matthau, Anthony Franciosa, Lee Remick. 1957, B&W, 125 minutes. A drunken hick rises to be a folksy network television singing star and then is revealed as a manipulative hypocrite intent on transforming his down-home charisma into political power. This early Hollywood whack at its television competition remains lively and full of surprises. Film debut of Griffith and Remick. Griffith character very loosely based on Arthur Godfrey. Not rated. Most appreciated by ages ten and over. (See page 81.)

■ **Fail-Safe.** Henry Fonda, Walter Matthau, Larry Hagman. 1964, B&W, 111 minutes. Peace-loving U.S. president (Fonda) works feverishly to find an international diplomatic solution when a U.S. aircraft is mistakenly dispatched to drop an H-Bomb on the Soviet Union. This film is one of several of the period (see *Dr. Strangelove* and *Seven Days in May*) designed to warn the public of the dangers of nuclear weapons. Hagman, later J. R. Ewing of television's "Dallas," plays a key presidential adviser. Not rated. Most appreciated by ages twelve and over. (See page 112.)

■ **Fat Man and Little Boy.** Paul Newman, Dwight Schultz, Bonnie Bedelia, John Cusack. 1989, color, 126 minutes. Scientists gather in the New Mexico desert, under the protective eye of U.S. Army officer Newman, to build the atomic bomb that will be dropped on Hiroshima, help end World War II, and usher in the nuclear age. Told in terms of human melodrama. Rated PG-13 for mature themes and oblique sexual situations.. Most appreciated by ages twelve and over. (See page 87.)

■ **First Monday in October.** Walter Matthau, Jill Clayburgh, Barnard Hughes, Jan Sterling. 1981, color, 98 minutes. The first woman Supreme Court justice (Clayburgh), a staunch conservative, does ferocious ideological battle with the court's leading liberal (Matthau) over the issue of First Amendment protection of pornographers. This unprecedented (for Hollywood) behind-the-scenes look at the high court handles its sensitive subject matter with balanced intelligence and good-humored bantering. Rated R for profanity and sexual content, although the sexual material is brief and handled with good taste. With this in mind, recommended for ages twelve and over. (See page 113.)

■ **Frankenstein.** Boris Karloff, Mae Clarke, Colin Clive. 1931, B&W, 70 minutes. Dr. Henry Frankenstein (Clive), obsessed with creating life in his castle laboratory, unknowingly implants a stolen "abnormal brain" in his latest experiment. A sixty-year-old classic as fresh now as the day it debuted. Karloff is sublime as the mythic monster. Not rated. Recommended for all ages. (See page 46.)

■ **Front Page, The.** Adolphe Menjou, Pat O'Brien, Edward Everett Horton, Mae Clarke. 1931, B&W, 103 minutes. This dog-eared drama of big-town journalism was a Broadway hit, then the basis for four movies, and still a staple of summer stock theater. The story concerns an escaped convict and a reporter who is trying to leave the business but ends up with the biggest story of his career. Romance and intraprofessional relationships accompany the quick-stepping story. The less appealing 1974 version stars Jack Lemmon, Walter Matthau, and Carol Burnett. In the 1940's *His Girl Friday,* one male lead was rewritten as a woman's part, to great comic effect. This switch was left intact in 1988's *Switching Channels,* but the context was changed to a television newsroom. Not rated. Recommended for all ages. (See page 105.)

■ **Gandhi.** Ben Kingsley, Candice Bergen, Edward Fox, John Gielgud, Trevor Howard, John Mills, Martin Sheen. 1982, color, 188 minutes. This ambitious biography of the inspirational leader who steered India to independence from Britain following World War II, and subsequently became the international symbol of nonviolent protest, depicts momentous historical events without losing touch with the mild-mannered, devout lawyer at their center. This Oscar winner may be the film world's most sensible treatment of Third World political-social currents, with a sparkling performance by Anglo-Indian actor Kingsley. Oscars: Best picture, director (Richard Attenborough), actor (Kingsley). Rated PG. Most appreciated by ages twelve and over. (See page 57.)

■ **Glenn Miller Story, The.** James Stewart, June Allyson, Harry (Henry) Morgan, Frances Langford, Louis Armstrong, Gene Krupa. 1954, color, 116 minutes. Trombonist Miller (Stewart) was one of the first to break the mold of big band blandness and help usher in the swing era in the 1920s and 1930s, on his way to becoming a popular composer and orchestra leader. This film biography hits the right notes in recounting Miller's career, cut short when he perished while touring Allied bases during World War II. Includes a tasty sampling of Miller standards. Not rated. Recommended for all ages. (See page 93.)

■ **Gold Rush, The.** Charlie Chaplin, Georgia Hale. 1925, B&W, 82 minutes. Most famous of Chaplin's classic silent comedies, has his Little Tramp character befriending a dance-hall girl, battling evil prospectors, and coping with arduous frozen Yukon conditions. *This* is what the Chaplin legend is all about. Not rated. Recommended for all ages. (See page 37.)

■ **Godzilla.** Raymond Burr. 1956, B&W, 80 minutes. A four-hundred-foot relic of the Jurassic Age, awakened by Pacific A-bomb tests, terrorizes modern Japan. A poorly dubbed Japanese-made monster classic, with additional U.S. footage grafted on, that is as funny as it is scary. Special effects showing the big guy tearing up what is meant to be downtown Tokyo are especially memorable. Not rated. Recommended for all ages. (See page 48.)

■ **Goodbye Girl, The.** Richard Dreyfuss, Marsha Mason, Quinn Cummings, Paul Benedict. 1977, color, 110 minutes. Aspiring actor Dreyfuss lands in comically bizarre living arrangement with ex-Broadway dancer Mason and her precocious daughter Cummings. Neil Simon comedy (written as a vehicle for then-wife Mason) offers a fetching love story, gentle satire of theater life, and plenty of his trademark wisecracks. Oscar: Best actor (Dreyfuss). Rated PG for moderate sexual situations. Recommended for all ages. (See page 42.)

■ **Greatest Show on Earth, The.** Charlton Heston, Betty Hutton, James Stewart, Cornel Wilde, Gloria Grahame, Dorothy Lamour. 1952, color, 153 minutes. Catchall panoply of life under and behind the big top, directed by the grand master of cinema spectacle, Cecil B. DeMille. Heston is the circus boss, Hutton his aerialist girlfriend, and Stewart the show's top clown. Oscar: Best picture. Not rated. Recommended for all ages. (See page 78.)

■ **Grey Fox, The.** Richard Farnsworth, Jackie Burroughs, Ken Pogue. 1982, color, 92 minutes. Wild West stagecoach robber Bill Miner is released after thirty-plus years in jail and adapts to the changing world by learning to rob trains. Real-life story with a rare combination of action, wit, and bemused social commentary. Rated PG for minimal, infrequent violence. Recommended for all ages. (See page 75.)

■ **Guess Who's Coming to Dinner.** Spencer Tracy, Katharine Hepburn, Sidney Poitier, Katharine Houghton. 1967, color, 108 minutes. Nice suburban liberal couple (Tracy, Hepburn) has their world turned upside down when their daughter (Hepburn's niece Houghton) brings home her new black boyfriend (Poitier) and announces their intention to get married. This bold and controversial movie was released at the height of U.S. racial tensions in the 1960s and caused a substantial stir on all sides of the issue. Holds up remarkably well as a sensitive drama of clashing cultures and emotions. Tracy died two weeks after the film's completion. Oscar: Best actress (Hepburn). Not rated. Recommended for all ages. (See page 54.)

■ **Gunfight at the OK Corral.** Burt Lancaster, Kirk Douglas, Rhonda Fleming, Jo Van Fleet, John Ireland, Lee Van Cleef. 1957, color, 122 minutes. Big-budget, big-star version of an often told western tale, with Lancaster as Tombstone marshal Wyatt Earp and Douglas as his rummy buddy Doc Holliday. An interesting case of American mythologizing, as more than two hours are spent relating the story of an incident that reportedly lasted thirty seconds. See also *My Darling Clementine.* Not rated. Recommended for all ages. (See page 70.)

■ **Hail the Conquering Hero.** Eddie Bracken, William Demarest, Ella Raines, Franklin Pangborn. 1944, B&W, 101 minutes. U.S. Marine recruit Bracken lets hometown citizens believe that he's a war hero when he can't bring himself to tell his mother (Raines) that he was released from service on a medical discharge. Townspeople are awestruck and urge him to run for mayor. Against-the-grain writer/director Preston Sturges pokes loving fun at unthinking hero worship and scores countless hits. Not rated. Recommended for all ages. (See page 38.)

■ **Hard Day's Night, A.** George Harrison, John Lennon, Paul McCartney, Ringo Starr, Wilfrid Brambell, Norman Rossington, Victor Spinetti. 1964, B&W, 85 minutes. Brilliantly innovative film by director Richard Lester, taking the convention of the celebrity-showcase movie and retooling it as a documentary-style excursion into pop cult madness. Goes a long, long way in capturing the essence of everything the Beatles represented. A jubilant way to show kids what the sixties were (in part) about. Not rated. Recommended for all ages. (See page 97.)

■ **Heart Is a Lonely Hunter, The.** Alan Arkin, Sondra Locke, Stacy Keach, Cicely Tyson, Percy Rodriquez. 1968, color, 125 minutes. Deaf-mute Arkin touches the lives of several individuals in a small southern town, most notably drifter Keach, black doctor Rodriquez, and precocious teen Locke. Weighty, intense drama of people transformed by a speechless man — whose own pain they cannot know — builds to a powerful finale. Movie debuts of Locke and Keach. Not rated. Most appreciated by ages twelve and over. (See page 63.)

■ **Heartland.** Rip Torn, Conchata Ferrell, Megan Folson, Barry Primus, Lilia Skala. 1979, color, 96 minutes. A Denver widow and her young daughter travel to Wyoming in 1910 to keep house for a cantankerous bachelor rancher and experience a litany of hardships on the rugged frontier. Based on the journals of frontierswoman Elinor Stewart, this is a treasure of a film that would have likely been lost to public viewing were it not for video. Simple, moving, ennobling, humbling — the story packs a mighty punch. Rated PG. Recommended for all ages. (See page 69.)

■ **Help!** George Harrison, John Lennon, Paul McCartney, Ringo Starr, Leo McKern, Eleanor Bron, Victor Spinetti. 1965, color, 90 minutes. The Beatles' second movie is more a traditional comedy than was the documentary-style *A Hard Day's Night,* with the boys fleeing religious cultists trying to pry a sacred ring away from Ringo. Not quite the second coming of the Marx Brothers (as some proposed at the time), but Groucho, Harpo, and Chico couldn't sing like this. Not rated. Recommended for all ages. (See page 97.)

■ **High Noon.** Gary Cooper, Grace Kelly, Lloyd Bridges. 1952, B&W, 84 minutes. Highly allegorical Western has frontier town sheriff Cooper about to retire to farming with new bride Kelly, but forced into one final confrontation with revenge-minded trio of desperadoes. Filmed at the height of the McCarthy era, with the townspeople's indifference to Cooper's crisis seen as a message to the public as to what might happen if good citizens did not stand up to the senator from Wisconsin. Solid picture, despite the heavy baggage. Oscar: Best actor (Cooper). Not rated. Recommended for all ages. (See page 69.)

■ **His Girl Friday.** Cary Grant, Rosalind Russell, Ralph Bellamy, Gene Lockhart. 1940, B&W, 92 minutes. Fast-paced adaptation of *The Front Page* retools the legendary newspaper drama as a raucous gender-clash comedy, transforming the Hildy Johnson role into a woman's part and having her be the ex-wife of stuffy publisher Walter Burns. Russell and Grant execute the switcheroo in fall-down funny style without losing the original's biting take on raucous prewar journalism. Not rated. Recommended for all ages. (See page 105.)

■ **Home of the Brave.** James Edwards, Lloyd Bridges, Frank Lovejoy, Steve Brodie. 1949, B&W, 85 minutes. A black GI is assigned to an all-white patrol on a clandestine mission to map a Japanese-held Pacific island, preparatory to U.S. invasion. This boldly confrontational film places its race-relations conflict in an explosive, super-macho setting — wartime combat — and straightforwardly deals with issues of prejudice, suspicion, and stereotypes. Not rated. Most appreciated by ages fourteen and over. (See page 52.)

■ **Honeysuckle Rose.** Willie Nelson, Dyan Cannon, Amy Irving, Slim Pickens. 1980, color, 119 minutes. Nelson plays a country and western singer in a light, fun, tune-filled commentary on life as a professional artist. It's mostly about the rigors of touring and the performing group as an extended family. Nelson fans will be delighted, and nonfans (plus the uninitiated) will be pleasantly surprised. Cannon does her own singing as Nelson's wife. Rated PG for moderate sexual situations. Recommended for all ages. (See page 95.)

■ **Hope and Glory.** Sarah Miles, Ian Bannen, Sammi Davis, Sebastian Rice-Edwards. 1987, color, 113 minutes. Coming of age amid the stress and ruin of wartime London, young Rice-Edwards's story begins in September 1939 with the Nazi invasion of Poland and the reflective observation that "nothing would ever be the same again." His experiences include air raids, bomb shelters, fear of gas attacks, downed German pilots, a father away at war, and the destruction of the family home. Director John Boorman's highly personal account most successfully captures the consequences of wartime childhood. Rated PG-13 for occasional violence and sexual content. Most appreciated by ages twelve and over. (See page 103.)

■ **Hud.** Patricia Neal, Paul Newman, Melvyn Douglas, Brandon DeWilde. 1963, B&W, 112 minutes. Rancher Douglas's hell-raising son Hud (Newman) conspires to take away his ranch while making life a living hell for housekeeper Neal and nephew DeWilde. Bitter, hyperrealistic soap-opera is largely told through the worshipful eyes of teenager DeWilde, as he slowly realizes that his fun-loving Uncle Hud is not the ideal role-model he once had thought. Oscars: Best actress (Neal), supporting actor (Douglas). Not rated. Most appreciated by ages fourteen and over. (See page 102.)

■ **Iceman.** Timothy Hutton, Lindsay Crouse, Danny Glover, John Lone. 1984, color, 99 minutes. Young scientists at an Arctic oil exploration site discover a Neanderthal man frozen in glacial ice, manage to bring him back to life, and then put him (figuratively) under a microscope to learn who he is and what he was. Engaging mix of medical mystery and anthropological drama that successfully educates as it entertains. Rated PG for infrequent profanity. Recommended for all ages. (See page 88.)

■ **In the Heat of the Night.** Rod Steiger, Sidney Poitier, Warren Oates, Lee Grant, Scott Wilson. 1967, color, 109 minutes. Poitier is a black northern cop just passing through a generic southern town, when a murder is committed and he becomes an immediate suspect. Popular film of the civil rights era plays well as both a crime-mystery thriller and a racial commentary. Oscars: Best picture, actor (Steiger). Not rated. Recommended for all ages. (See page 54.)

■ **Inherit the Wind.** Spencer Tracy, Fredric March, Gene Kelly, Harry Morgan, Dick York. 1960, B&W, 127 minutes. Dramatization of landmark Scopes "monkey trial," with Tennessee schoolteacher (York) prosecuted for lecturing on Darwinism and violating state taboo on teaching anything but biblical creationism. Dramatic sparks provided by courtroom combatants Tracy and March in characters based on real-life Scopes adversaries Clarence Darrow and William Jennings Bryan. Not rated. Most appreciated by ages ten and over. (See page 90.)

■ **Invasion of the Body Snatchers.** Kevin McCarthy, Dana Wynter, Larry Gates, Carolyn Jones. 1956, B&W, 80 minutes. Not rated. Remade: Donald Sutherland, Brooke Adams, Leonard Nimoy, Jeff Goldblum, Veronica Cartwright. 1978, color, 115 minutes. Rated PG. Mysterious pods infest quiet American town gestating exact replicas of the town's inhabitants – except that pod people have no thoughts or emotions. Exceptional psychological thriller uses implied intellectual threat instead of traditional violence as the source of its terror. The original offers slightly more pulse-pounding excitement and tension. Most appreciated by ages ten and over, and only then if the nightmare stage has passed. (See page 50.)

■ **Invisible Man, The.** Claude Rains, Gloria Stuart, William Harrigan, Henry Travers. 1933, B&W, 71 minutes. Scientist Rains experiments with a rare drug that makes him invisible, only to discover it also transforms him into a deranged, power-mad murderer. H. G. Wells's science-gone-amok fantasy is rendered in a tidy little thriller with eye-popping special effects. The screen debut for Rains. That kindly gent (Travers) playing Dr. Claypool was later to appear as the angel Clarence in *It's a Wonderful Life.* Not rated. Recommended for all ages. (See page 86.)

■ **Jaws.** Roy Scheider, Robert Shaw, Richard Dreyfuss, Lorraine Gary, Murray Hamilton. 1975, color, 124 minutes. Killer white shark terrorizes summer bathers at a popular Northeast coastal resort, as town fathers downplay the menace for fear of driving away tourists. An uncommonly well-made scary-creature movie that gets better (and no less scarier) with each viewing. Followed by three sequels, none of merit. Rated PG for infrequent violence. Recommended for all ages who can still get to sleep and love the beach after watching a killer shark rampage for two hours. (See page 48.)

■ **Jeremiah Johnson.** Robert Redford, Will Geer. 1972, color, 107 minutes. Rugged young Johnson (Redford) turns his back on nineteenth-century civilization and learns to live alone in the Rocky Mountain wilderness, dealing with starvation, vengeful Indians, brutish soldiers, rival hunters, and other hardships. The movies' most successful depiction of the mystique of the mountain men of western folklore. Rated PG for infrequent violence. Recommended for all ages. (See page 71.)

■ **Johnny Belinda.** Jane Wyman, Lew Ayres, Charles Bickford, Agnes Moorehead, Stephen McNally. 1948, B&W, 103 minutes. Deaf-mute farm girl (Wyman) living in a desolate island community is given new hope when the town doctor (Ayres) teaches her lip-reading and sign language. This landmark film is pleasing to watch and brilliantly performed. A deeply touching human melodrama with real substance at its core. Oscar: Best actress (Wyman). Recommended for all ages. (See page 63.)

■ **Judgment at Nuremberg.** Spencer Tracy, Maximilian Schell, Burt Lancaster, Marlene Dietrich, Richard Widmark, Judy Garland, Montgomery Clift, William Shatner. 1961, B&W, 178 minutes. A post-World War II U.S. tribunal hears the American military's case against four German judges who had dutifully enforced Nazi law. Soaring, sharply intelligent courtroom drama explores the complex issue of judicial responsibility in the context of Third Reich horror stories without losing its emotional impact. Rarely has a clash of ideas and philosophies been captured more dramatically on film. Not rated. Most appreciated by ages ten and over. (See page 91.)

■ **King Kong.** Fay Wray, Robert Armstrong, Bruce Cabot. 1933, B&W/colorized, 100 minutes. A film crew travels to an uncharted East Indies island to film a legendary monster ape, then brings the beast back to New York City in hopes of making a fortune from his sensational public display. Alas, Kong gets loose in midtown Manhattan, and you'll never look at the Empire State Building the same way again. The special effects are still dazzling, and the gargantuan ape is one of the screen's most sympathetic creature terrors. Not rated. Recommended for all ages. (See page 47.)

■ **King of Comedy, The.** Robert DeNiro, Jerry Lewis, Sandra Bernhard. 1983, color, 109 minutes. Pathetic, no-account celebrity groupie Rupert Pupkin (DeNiro) is so convinced of his own talents that he kidnaps a popular television talk show host (Lewis) to prove his skills and secure his big break. Cleverly satiric commentary on the perils and whims of being a celebrity, with knock-out performances by DeNiro and Lewis and an ending that is truly inspired. Rated PG. Most appreciated by ages ten and over. (See page 78.)

■ **Knock on Any Door.** Humphrey Bogart, John Derek. 1949, B&W, 100 minutes. A 1940s youth crime melodrama, with slum kid Derek involved in a cop killing and do-gooder attorney Bogart coming to his defense. Marks the transition from the movies' tough-but-harmless street punks of the 1930s to the slicker, meaner juvenile delinquents of the 1950s – and today. Not rated. Most appreciated by ages ten and over. (See page 43.)

■ **La Bamba.** Lou Diamond Phillips, Elizabeth Pena. 1987, color, 108 minutes. Hispanic rocker Richie Valens (Phillips) lived just long enough to have a couple of hit songs and make a statement about his people's rightful place in the rock mainstream. Important story told with appropriate energy, intensity, and flair. Phillips's film debut. Rated PG-13 for infrequent profanity and sexual content. Most appreciated by ages ten and over. (See page 96.)

■ **Last Hurrah, The.** Spencer Tracy, Pat O'Brien, Jeffrey Hunter, Basil Rathbone, John Carradine. 1958, B&W, 111 minutes. Popular Irish Catholic mayor confronts the fact that his patronage-based political machine is a thing of the past, then launches one last reelection campaign. This sentimental tribute to big-city bosses is loosely based on Boston mayor James Michael Curley (whose unofficial campaign slogan was "Vote Often, Vote Early, for James Michael Curley"). Director John Ford shows off his eye for capturing out-of-the-way pockets of ethnic culture. Not rated. Most appreciated by ages twelve and over. (See page 108.)

■ **Lawrence of Arabia.** Peter O'Toole, Omar Sharif, Alec Guinness, Anthony Quinn, Arthur Kennedy, Jack Hawkins, Claude Rains, Anthony Quayle, Jose Ferrer. 1962, color, 216 minutes. British officer T. E. Lawrence rallies Arab tribesmen to drive the Turks from their desert lands during World War I, only to have Arabia become a political pawn when the European powers divvy up the

Middle East at war's end. The best big-screen epic ever loses some impact on video, but the scope of the human and political drama is undiminished. Reissued in 1989 in letter-box video format, with added material and some cuts. Oscars: Best picture, director (David Lean). Not rated. Recommended for all ages. (See page 55.)

■ **Let It Be.** George Harrison, John Lennon, Paul McCartney, Ringo Starr, Yoko Ono. 1970, color, 80 minutes. Documentary narrative of the recording of the Beatles' final album and their last public appearance together in an impromptu concert atop the recording studio. Unexceptional filmmaking, but this is *history*. Rated G. Recommended for all ages. (See page 97.)

■ **Lillies of the Field.** Sidney Poitier, Lilia Skala. 1963, B&W, 93 minutes. Spare, affecting melodrama of an itinerant black handyman (Poitier) taken in by Catholic sisters of a desert convent and the life lessons they learn from each other. Hollywood at its best, presenting basic morality lessons in a simple, believable story. Oscar: Best actor (Poitier). Not rated. Recommended for all ages. (See page 52.)

■ **Little Big Man.** Dustin Hoffman, Faye Dunaway, Martin Balsam, Chief Dan George. 1970, color, 150 minutes. Ancient, shriveled Jack Crabb (Hoffman), last living survivor of Custer's Battle at Little Big Horn, recalls his long, eventful frontier life growing up with and around Native Americans. One of the first and most aggressively pro-Indian Hollywood products. Tries to mix broad humor with its sensitive drama, not always with success. Commentaries on the white man by Old Lodgeskins (played by Chief Dan George) are majestic and unforgettable. Rated PG. Most appreciated by ages ten and over. (See page 73.)

■ **Lonely Are the Brave.** Kirk Douglas, Gena Rowlands, Walter Matthau. 1962, B&W, 107 minutes. Contemporary cowboy Douglas, feeling hemmed in by modern society, breaks out of jail and heads for the New Mexico hills on horseback, pursued by a high-tech posse and sympathetic sheriff (Matthau). A notable effort to depict social dysfunction of aging through the experience of geriatric cowboys. Not rated. Most appreciated by ages twelve and over. (See page 74.)

■ **Lord of the Flies.** 1963, B&W, 90 minutes. Film version of William Golding's grim allegory of civilization on the edge. Features a cast of unknown youthful performers as early 20th century schoolboys marooned on a tropical island, with many of them reverting to prehistoric savagery and becoming predatory killers. Is this the human condition? Watch it and decide. Not rated. A few violent scenes. Most appreciated by ages ten and over. (Remade in color and "modernized" to no good effect in 1990, in an R-rated version that is not recommended.) (See page 99.)

■ **Love Me or Leave Me.** Doris Day, James Cagney, Cameron Mitchell. 1955, color, 122 minutes. Jazz singer Ruth Etting (Day) makes it to the top of the heap, with the help of a Chicago gangster nicknamed "The Gimp" (Cagney). One of the best musical film bios sugarcoats a rather steamy (and seamy) story. Day sings thirteen Etting standards with sublime style. Not rated. Most appreciated by ages ten and up. (See page 94.)

■ **MacArthur.** Gregory Peck, Dan O'Herlihy, Ed Flanders. 1977. color, 130 minutes. Reverential biography of the controversial World War II and Korean War commander focuses as much on its subject's peacetime activities – including his stint as postwar military governor of Japan – as his triumphant generalship. An important figure in a responsible, if sometimes plodding, film treatment. Rated PG. Recommended for all ages. (See page 58.)

■ **Man Called Horse, A.** Richard Harris, Judith Anderson, Manu Tupou. 1970. color, 114 minutes. An English nobleman trekking through the American West after the Civil War is kidnapped by Sioux tribesmen and gradually is adopted by tribal leaders. Virtually the same plot as *Dances with Wolves* and offering even more intelligent, sensitive, and original insights into Native American culture. Harris was to spearhead the production of two recommended sequels, *Return of a Man Called Horse* and *Triumphs of a Man Called Horse.* Rated PG for infrequent violence. Recommended for all ages. (See page 72.)

■ **Man Who Shot Liberty Valance, The.** James Stewart, John Wayne, Vera Miles, Lee Marvin, Andy Devine, Woody Strode. 1962, B&W, 119 minutes. The Wild West's sometimes bloody transition from lawlessness to civility is told in the story of a young eastern lawyer (Stewart) whose reluctant rise to political prominence is sparked by his helping to gun down a notorious outlaw. This impressively comprehensive Western embodies several strains of American frontier mythology. A picture that rewards repeat viewings. Not rated. Recommended for all ages. (See page 67.)

■ **Marie.** Sissy Spacek, Jeff Daniels, Morgan Freeman, Fred Thompson. 1985, color, 112 minutes. Tennessee housewife Marie Ragghianti (Spacek) is nominated to the state parole board and becomes embroiled in a controversial fight against executive-office corruption. Impassioned drama is based on Ragghianti's real-life experiences (which led to the imprisonment of the Tennessee governor), powerfully interpreted by Spacek. Rated PG-13 for infrequent violence and profanity. Most appreciated by ages twelve and over. (See page 84.)

■ **Mask.** Cher, Eric Stoltz, Sam Elliot, Laura Dern, Richard Dysart. 1985, color, 120 minutes. Based on the true story of a young teenager, Rocky Dennis (Stoltz), born with a rare disease that causes his skull to grow to grotesque proportions, giving his face the appearance of a mask. Rocky and his mom (Cher) hang out with a rough-and-tough motorcycle gang who are more tolerant of Rocky's disfigurement than so-called mainstream society. That's just one of the many offbeat twists to this warm, sensitive, winning depiction of an especially formidable type of physical challenge. Rated PG-13 for infrequent harsh profanity and sexual discussions. Highly recommended for family viewing, as Rocky's family unit is rare and strong, and his character is one of such transcendent beauty. Most appreciated by ages ten and over. (See page 65.)

■ **Member of the Wedding, The.** Julie Harris, Brandon DeWilde, Ethel Waters. 1952, B&W, 91 minutes. Motherless twelve-year-old Frankie Adams (Harris) looks for love, friendship, and familial warmth in a stirring adaptation of Carson McCullers's popular rites-of-passage novel and play of the same name. Exceptional screen-debut performance by Harris (who was actually twenty-seven at the time!) and DeWilde. Not rated. Most appreciated by ages twelve and over. (See page 101.)

■ **Milagro Beanfield War, The.** Chick Vennera, Ruben Blades, Sonia Braga, Melanie Griffith, Richard Bradford, Daniel Stern, Christopher Walken, M. Emmett Walsh. 1988, color, 117 minutes. Fed-up farmer Vennera strikes back at the New Mexico land developers who have usurped his ancestors' traditional water rights, thereby sparking a miniature revolt that soon reaches all the way to the statehouse. This underappreciated movie is rich in visual texture, musical score, plot detail, and supporting characters. Denigrated by critics waiting for director Robert Redford to fail. He doesn't. Rated R for infrequent violence and profanity. Recommended for all ages with parental discretion. (See page 85.)

■ **Miracle of Morgan's Creek, The.** Eddie Bracken, Betty Hutton, William Demarest, Brian Donlevy, Akim Tamiroff. 1944, B&W, 99 minutes. Small-town, big-dream girl Hutton finds herself pregnant after an all-night party at the nearby Army base but has no idea who the father is. Good-hearted suitor Bracken comes to her rescue, getting more than he bargained for. Genius comedy director Preston Sturges takes on American mores in this high-spirited farce. One of the great ones. Not rated. Most appreciated by ages twelve and over. (See page 38.)

■ **Miracle Worker, The.** Anne Bancroft, Patty Duke, Victor Jory, Inga Swenson, Andrew Prine. 1962, B&W, 107 minutes. Bright young Helen Keller (Duke), blind and deaf since infancy, is an increasing burden to her family until her father secures the services of a remarkable teacher — herself functionally blind — named Annie Sullivan (Bancroft). Inspired by Keller's autobiography and based on a Broadway play (and originally a live television drama), the profoundly moving film covers the first few weeks of the tempestuous Keller-Sullivan relationship. Oscars: Best actress (Bancroft), supporting actress (Duke). Not rated. Highly recommended for all ages. (See page 62.)

■ **Modern Times.** Charles Chaplin, Paulette Goddard, Chester Conklin. 1936, B&W, 89 minutes. Chaplin's Little Tramp confronts contemporary society in the form of dehumanizing industrial factories and labor-busting goons, and opts for an idyllic life with street waif Goddard. Definitive Chaplin film for its mix of laugh-out-loud comedy and provocative political commentary. Not rated. Recommended for all ages. (See page 36.)

■ **Mosquito Coast, The.** Harrison Ford, Helen Mirren, River Phoenix, Martha Plimpton. 1986, color, 117 minutes. Eccentric inventor Ford uproots his family and moves to a remote Central American jungle village, where he can create the perfect existence and play benevolent god to the natives – and his children. An overlooked masterpiece that probes the dark heart of family love, loyalty, and obedience. Rated PG. Recommended for all ages. (See page 102.)

■ **Mr. Smith Goes to Washington.** James Stewart, Jean Arthur, Claude Rains. 1939, B&W, 129 minutes. Idealistic young Stewart is plucked from obscurity and appointed to fill a U.S. Senate seat. Before long, he becomes the national leader of a battle against Washington corruption. A strikingly frank view of official Washington that balances its contempt for entrenched political hacks with the nobility of Stewart's idealism. Includes one of Stewart's most famous movie scenes – an impassioned all-night filibuster against a scandalous government land grab. Not rated. Most appreciated by ages ten and over. (See page 111.)

■ **My Darling Clementine.** Henry Fonda, Victor Mature, Linda Darnell, Walter Brennan, Tim Holt, Ward Bond. 1946, B&W, 97 minutes. Legendary gunfight at Tombstone's OK Corral between the Earp brothers and the desperado Clanton boys has been the subject of several movies, none better than this John Ford jewel. As clear and crisp as the desert air, this understated movie triumph succeeds in convincing viewers that this is Western frontier life as it really was. Walter Brennan, usually found playing lovable old coots, is the picture of snarly meanness as Pa Clanton. Not rated. Recommended for all ages. (See page 70.)

■ **My Life as a Dog.** Anton Glanzelius. 1985, color, 101 minutes. Mischevious youngster Glanzelius loses his mother and must leave the city to live with relatives in a remote village, where he experiences his early sexual and spiritual awakening – all the while likening his life to a Soviet space dog, Leika, who perpetually circles the earth in someone else's orbit. This popular Swedish film offers a charming, poignant take on the wonders and tragedies of childhood, with a captivating performance by young Glanzelius. Not rated. Infrequent sexual dialogue. Most appreciated by ages twelve and over. (See page 101.)

■ **My Favorite Year.** Peter O'Toole, Mark Linn-Baker, Joseph Bologna, Lainie Kazan, Bill Macy, Jessica Harper. 1982, color, 92 minutes. Zany comedy of the early days of network television, with scriptwriter Linn-Baker baby-sitting notorious bad-boy actor O'Toole before his scheduled appearance on Bologna's variety show. One of the funniest movies of the past twenty-five years, it's also a dandy window on the wildly creative spontaneity of 1950s live television (Bologna's show is based on Sid Caesar's hit series "Your Show of Shows"). Rated PG. Recommended for all ages. (See page 42.)

■ **My Left Foot.** Daniel Day-Lewis, Brenda Fricker, Fiona Shaw, Ray McAnally, Hugh O'Conor, Cyril Cusack. 1989, color, 103 minutes. Much-honored film biography of Irish painter/poet Christy Brown (Day-Lewis), born with cerebral palsy and limited in movement to his left foot. Engrossing human-interest tale succeeds in greatly humanizing Brown, steering his triumphant story away from soppy melodrama and into the realm of noble and exhilarating personal achievement. Raw, rich, and earthy – a delight that will thrill viewers of all ages. O'Conor is a wonder as young Christy. Oscars: Best actor (Day-Lewis), supporting actress (Fricker). Rated R for infrequent profanity and indirect sexual references. Recommended for all ages with parental discretion. (See page 64.)

■ **Nashville.** Henry Gibson, Lily Tomlin, Keith Carradine, Karen Black, Ronee Blakely, Geraldine Chaplin, Michael Murphy, Ned Beatty, Keenan Wynn, Scott Glenn, Barbara Harris, Shelley Duvall. 1975, color, 159 minutes. Multiple plots intertwine backstage at the country music capital, with director Robert Altman holding up Nashville as a mirror for the rest of the country to look into. The primary story is about a southern populist presidential candidate (never seen on-screen) and the assassin stalking him. The stars not only sing their own songs, but many also wrote the lyrics. Rated R for infrequent profanity and violence. Most appreciated by ages twelve and over. (See page 77.)

■ **Night at the Opera, A.** Groucho, Chico, and Harpo Marx; Kitty Carlisle; Margaret Dumont; Allan Jones. 1935, B&W, 92 minutes. More than mere Marx Brothers comedy, this top-drawer effort has a sweet romance between Carlisle and Jones and some tunes of real quality – plus, of course, some of the brothers' most inspired lunacy. Not rated. Recommended for all ages. (See page 36.)

■ **Norma Rae.** Sally Field, Ron Leibman, Beau Bridges, Pat Hingle. 1979, color, 113 minutes. Textile mill worker Field is transformed into an activist union organizer and suffers social ostracism in her small southern hometown. One of the first major pictures to present a woman in the traditionally male rebel-with-a-cause role. Oscar: Best actress (Field). Rated PG. Recommended for all ages. (See page 84.)

■ **Nothing Sacred.** Carole Lombard, Fredric March, Walter Connolly. 1937, B&W, 75 minutes. Scoop-hungry New York reporter March attempts to exploit the tearjerker story of supposedly fatally ill Lombard, only to find she's using him to become a Gotham celebrity. Supercynical comedy about fast-and-loose journalism, not unlike that practiced by today's steamier tabloids. Lombard was the premier comedienne of the 1930s, and here we see why. Not rated. Most appreciated by ages ten and over. (See page 105.)

■ **Odd Couple, The.** Jack Lemmon, Walter Matthau. 1968, color, 105 minutes. Fussy, fastidious Felix Unger (Lemmon) breaks up with his wife and moves in with his sloppy sportswriter pal Oscar Madison (Matthau), setting off one of the most uproarious domestic comedies ever written. This well-traveled Neil Simon creation was a hit as a play on Broadway and later as a long-running television series starring Tony Randall (Felix) and Jack Klugman (Oscar). For all that, it's never lost its freshness and bounce. Not rated. Recommended for all ages. (See page 41.)

■ **On the Waterfront.** Marlon Brando, Eva Marie Saint, Karl Malden, Rod Steiger, Lee J. Cobb. 1954, B&W, 108 minutes. Gripping, gritty drama of an ex-boxer's solitary fight against corrupt union bosses on New York's waterfront and his love for the daughter of working-class parents who is trying to escape her environment. Ennobling underdog cinema and an excellent introduction to the charismatic Brando's screen work. Oscars: Best picture, best director (Elia Kazan), best actor (Brando), best supporting actress (Saint). Not rated. Most appreciated by ages ten and over. (See page 83.)

■ **Other Side of the Mountain, The.** Marilyn Hassett, Beau Bridges, Dabney Coleman. 1975, color, 101 minutes. Probable 1956 Olympic ski team member Jill Kinmont (Hassett) is critically injured in her final qualifying race and must face life as a wheelchair-bound quadriplegic. Traditional tearjerker rescued by an articulate rage at the mistreatment of handicapped people in society. Followed by a comparable 1978 sequel, *The Other Side of the Mountain, Part 2* (color, 100 minutes). Both rated PG and recommended for all ages. (See page 66.)

■ **Outlaw Josey Wales, The.** Clint Eastwood, Chief Dan George, Sandra Locke, Sam Bottoms. 1976, color, 135 minutes. Peaceable border-state farmer (Eastwood) is drawn into the Civil War when marauding Union troops slaughter his family. Tough, bitter Western dealing with the character of the vengeful vigilante and the lawless turmoil of the wartime frontier. Eastwood's first Western as a director (and last Western until 1985's *Pale Rider*). Rated PG for violence. Recommended for all ages. (See page 71.)

■ **Patton.** George C. Scott, Karl Malden. 1970, color, 169 minutes. Among the best screen biographies ever, the lengthy, historically comprehensive spectacular succeeds by never losing sight of its fascinating central character: a chivalrous, anachronistic American military leader of World War II. The film traces Patton's triumphal, often tumultuous wartime career through the conquest of Sicily and the race across Europe to defeat Germany. Scott is spellbinding. Oscars: Best picture, director (Franklin Schaffner), actor (Scott; award refused). Rated PG for moderate, infrequent violence. Recommended for all ages. (See page 57.)

■ **Philadelphia Story, The.** Katharine Hepburn, Cary Grant, James Stewart, Roland Young, Ruth Hussey. 1940, B&W, 112 minutes. Lovely, elegant comedy of manners and morals featuring the hot-and-cold romance of Tracy Lord (Hepburn) and Dexter Haven (Grant). Grandly stylish, outrageously funny, and brilliantly performed. A must-see entertainment event. Not rated. Some adult themes may be lost on younger children, but all the great screen comedies have something for everyone. (See page 37.)

■ **Pink Panther Strikes Again, The.** Peter Sellers, Lesley-Anne Downe, Herbert Lom, Colin Blakely. 1976, color, 103 minutes. Inspector Clouseau's former boss (Lom) is out to destroy the world with a cosmic ray gun. Best of the Panther series and best physical comedy of the modern era. (See also *Return of the Pink Panther.*) Rated PG. Recommended for all ages. (See page 40.)

■ **Powwow Highway.** Gary Farmer, A. Martinez, Amanda Wyss. 1989, color, 90 minutes. Two young Cheyenne men — one a social activist, the other a keeper of tribal history and tradition — travel from their Colorado reservation to Santa Fe, discoursing as they go on their disparate views of contemporary Native American social roles. A bright, funny, and pleasingly trenchant road picture that provides a rare and rewarding look at modern Native American culture. Not rated. Most appreciated by ages twelve and over. (See page 74.)

■ **Producers, The.** Zero Mostel, Gene Wilder, Dick Shawn, Lee Meredith, Kenneth Mars. 1968, color, 88 minutes. Charlatan Broadway producer Mostel concocts a scheme, with the assistance of mousey accountant Wilder, to bilk rich widows by having them invest heavily in a musical (*Springtime for Hitler*) that is doomed to fail. Writer/director Mel Brooks's best comedy and one of the all-time best comedies of the modern movie era. Rated PG, with some oblique sexual repartee. Recommended for all ages. (See page 39.)

■ **Rain Man.** Dustin Hoffman, Tom Cruise, Valerie Golino. 1988, color, 140 minutes. Young wheeler-dealer Cruise, disinherited by his father, learns he has an autistic much-older brother (Hoffman), whom he "frees" from the institution where he's lived for twenty-three years. Highly sensitive presentation of psychiatric disabilities and the foundations of sibling love, as Cruise and Hoffman travel cross-country together. A film that grows with age and repeat viewings. Oscars: Best picture, director (Barry Levinson), actor (Hoffman). Rated R for harsh profanity and sexual situations. Most appreciated by ages ten and over. (See page 61.)

■ **Rebel without a Cause.** James Dean, Natalie Wood, Sal Mineo. 1955, color, 111 minutes. Teenager Dean combats parents, peers, and himself in his struggle to make peace with mainstream society. The quintessential rebellious-youth picture, a 1950s cultural time capsule, and the fountainhead of Dean's posthumous mythology. Something magical happens on-screen, and even today the film tends to stick with viewers forever. Not rated. Recommended for all ages. (See page 44.)

■ **Red Badge of Courage, The.** Audie Murphy, Royal Dano, Bill Mauldin, Andy Devine. 1951, B&W, 69 minutes. A youthful Union soldier gets his first horrific taste of battle in the Civil War. Brief, unforgettable adaptation of the Stephen Crane novel features former World War II hero Murphy (see *To Hell and Back*) and Mauldin, a Pulitzer Prize-winning newspaper cartoonist who got his start with *Stars and Stripes.* Not rated. Recommended for all ages. (See page 102.)

■ **Red River.** John Wayne, Montgomery Clift, Walter Brennan, Joanne Dru. 1948, B&W, 133 minutes. Texas rancher Wayne and adopted son Clift are forced by poor post-Civil War economic conditions to take their prized cattle hundreds of miles overland to market, initiating what would become the Chisholm Trail cattle drive. One of the half dozen definitive, must-see Westerns, this is a thinly disguised remake of *Mutiny on the Bounty,* with Wayne a tyrannical Captain Bligh and Clift a rebellious Fletcher Christian. Clift's debut film; Wayne's best Western. Not rated. Recommended for all ages. (See page 69.)

■ **Return of the Pink Panther.** Peter Sellers, Christopher Plummer, Catherine Schell, Herbert Lom. 1975, color, 113 minutes. Director Blake Edwards and actor Peter Sellers revive their Inspector Clouseau character — last seen in 1964's so-so *A Shot in the Dark* — to produce two of the best modern comedies. This was the first, and the next, *The Pink Panther Strikes Again,* was even better. Here Clouseau tracks down a slippery international jewel thief known as the Phantom (Plummer), but plot hardly matters in these hilarious escapades. Rated PG. Recommended for all ages. (See page 40.)

■ **Ride the High Country.** Randolph Scott, Joel McCrea, Mariette Hartley. 1962, color, 94 minutes. Two washed-up lawmen — one reduced to performing in carnival sideshows — sign on to escort a valuable gold shipment through outlaw country. A classic Western notable for its respectful, often witty commentary on growing old and the grizzled performances by 1940s Western B-movie stars McCrea and Scott. Not rated. Recommended for all ages. (See page 74.)

■ **Right Stuff, The.** Scott Glenn, Fred Ward, Ed Harris, Dennis Quaid, Sam Shepard, Barbara Hershey, Kim Stanley, Veronica Cartwright, Kathy Baker, Pamela Reed. 1983, color, 193 minutes. Stirring flag-waving docudrama of the early U.S. space program and the original "Mercury Seven" astronauts who flew the first U.S. manned space flights. This ambitious project, based on Tom Wolfe's nonfiction book, is successful in recreating epochal events and defining the distinctive personalities involved in the story. Rated PG for infrequent profanity. Recommended for all ages. (See page 58.)

■ **Saint Joan.** Jean Seberg, Richard Widmark, Richard Todd, John Gielgud, Harry Andrews. 1957, B&W/colorized, 110 minutes. Straightforward account of Joan of Arc's transformation from peasant girl to national leader and religious martyr. Most renowned for the debut of Seberg, cast in the much-coveted role after a highly publicized nationwide talent search. Not rated. Most appreciated by ages ten and over. (See page 59.)

■ **Separate But Equal.** Sidney Poitier, Burt Lancaster, Richard Kiley, Cleavon Little. 1991, color, 193 minutes. This grandly educational drama traces the route of a key school desegregation case up to the Supreme Court in the early 1950s. Poitier plays NAACP chief legal counsel (later Supreme Court justice) Thurgood Marshall; Lancaster plays his courtroom adversary (and former vice-presidential candidate) John W. Davis. Must viewing for those who wish to understand the roots of the civil rights movement. Not rated. Most appreciated by ages ten and over. (See page 54.)

■ **Sergeant York.** Gary Cooper, Walter Brennan, Joan Leslie, Ward Bond, Noah Beery, Jr., June Lockhart. 1941, B&W/colorized, 134 minutes. Soft-spoken Tennessee backwoodsman York (Cooper) sets aside his religious beliefs to fight in World War I and returns a great American hero. One of the best of the few Hollywood World War I dramas, it is also an effective, unadorned sermon on the values versus responsibilities tussle. Oscar: Best actor (Cooper). Not rated. Recommended for all ages. (See page 58.)

■ **Seven Days in May.** Burt Lancaster, Kirk Douglas, Ava Gardner, Fredric March, Edmond O'Brien, Martin Balsam. 1964, B&W, 120 minutes. Renegade right-wing U.S. military leaders plot to take over the White House and thwart the liberal president's campaign for a controversial nuclear disarmament treaty. Highly suspenseful, intellectual thriller gives a dramatic perspective on the interplay of institutional forces in official Washington. Reflects the hostile, confrontational politics of the Cold War era and the paranoia sweeping the land (the film was in preparation at the time of the Kennedy assassination). Not rated. Recommended for all ages (even though there is little actual "action," the fast pacing and vivid characters should keep even younger viewers enthralled). (See page 112.)

■ **Shane.** Alan Ladd, Jean Arthur, Van Heflin, Jack Palance, Brandon de Wilde. 1953, color, 118 minutes. A solitary figure rides into a frontier settlement and is thrust into a battle between sheep farmers claiming tracts of western prairie and the free-range ranchers who want to evict them. Ultimate presentation of the myth of the avenging angel as lone gunman, and high-relief drama of the economic forces at war on the frontier. Gorgeous to look at and great fun to watch. Among the most famous – and spine-tingling – final scenes ever filmed. Not rated. Recommended for all ages. (See page 68.)

■ **Shootist, The.** John Wayne, Lauren Bacall, James Stewart, Ron Howard, Richard Boone, Harry Morgan, Hugh O'Brian. 1976, color, 99 minutes. A reformed gunfighter (Wayne) confronting a terminal illness straps on his six-shooters for one last showdown with the bad guys. Affecting film made doubly moving by the fact that it is Wayne's final movie performance, made while he was fighting terminal cancer. Rated PG. Recommended for all ages. (See page 75.)

■ **Silkwood.** Meryl Streep, Cher, Kurt Russell, Ron Silver, Craig T. Nelson, Fred Ward, Diana Scarwid. 1983, color, 128 minutes. An employee of a nuclear fuel production plant becomes concerned at radiation risks to workers and begins cooperating with a national organization investigating nuclear safety hazards. The headline-making story of Karen Silkwood (Streep) is brought vividly to the screen through her on-the-job activism and home life with her boyfriend (Russell) and roommate (Cher). Rated R for infrequent profanity and sexual content. Most appreciated by ages twelve and over. (See page 84.)

■ **Singin' in the Rain.** Gene Kelly, Debbie Reynolds, Donald O'Connor, Jean Hagen. 1952, color, 102 minutes. A backstage look at Hollywood during the transition from silent pictures to talkies and how it affects the lives of a young singer (Reynolds), composer (O'Connor), and choreographer (Kelly). Consensus pick as the best movie musical ever. The one movie that every family should see at least once. Not rated. Recommended for all ages. (See page 79.)

■ **Some Like It Hot.** Jack Lemmon, Tony Curtis, Marilyn Monroe, Joe E. Brown, George Raft, Pat O'Brien. 1959, B&W, 119 minutes. Two Chicago musicians inadvertently witness the gangland shooting known as the St. Valentine's Day massacre and must flee for their lives, disguised as female members of an all-girl jazz band. This eyebrow-raising premise (Lemmon and Curtis are dressed as women for much of the movie) is executed with exquisite taste and exuberant comedy style. Marilyn Monroe, as the band's featured singer, delivers her most engaging screen performance. Not rated. Recommended for all ages. (See page 39.)

■ **Sounder.** Paul Winfield, Cicely Tyson, Kevin Hooks, Janet MacLachlan, Taj Mahal. 1972, color, 105 minutes. A black sharecropper (Winfield) is imprisoned for stealing meat to feed his impoverished family in 1930s Louisiana. His young son (Hooks) sets off to visit him, accompanied by the family hunting dog, Sounder. The popular novel is brought to the screen with achingly real performances by all and a splendid recreation of the story's time, place, and circumstance. Rated G. Recommended for all ages. (See page 100.)

■ **Spartacus.** Kirk Douglas, Laurence Olivier, Jean Simmons, Tony Curtis, Charles Laughton, Peter Ustinov, John Gavin, Nina Foch. 1960, color, 184 minutes (newly restored version released in 1991). A strong-willed gladiator (Douglas) leads a slave and peasant rebellion against the decadent leadership of republican Rome. A sterling example of blending human drama with lavish historical spectacle. The "I am Spartacus" scene captures the revolutionary spirit as well as any on screen. Oscar: Best supporting actor (Ustinov). Not rated. Recommended for all ages. (See page 56.)

■ **Spirit of St. Louis, The.** James Stewart, Patricia Smith, Murray Hamilton. 1957, color, 138 minutes. The inspirational story of Charles Lindbergh, the most celebrated American hero of the 1920s, focuses on preparations for his unprecedented New York-Paris solo flight and the flight itself. Despite being twenty-plus years older than the Lindbergh of 1927, Stewart carries the film with a typically gracious and subtly intellectual performance. Not rated. Recommended for all ages. (See page 57.)

■ **Stage Door.** Katharine Hepburn, Lucille Ball, Eve Arden, Ginger Rogers, Anne Miller, Adolphe Menjou, Franklin Pangborn. 1937, B&W, 92 minutes. Lively comings and goings in a New York City boarding house for aspiring young actresses mostly zero in on Rogers and Powell trying to make it as nightclub hoofers and wealthy, eccentric debutante Hepburn landing her first big dramatic role. Role provides Hepburn with one of her most famous film lines: "The calla lilies are in bloom again." A spunky, fun movie, with most of the laughs coming from pre-Lucy Ball and pre-Miss Brooks Arden. Not rated. Recommended for all ages. (See page 77.)

■ **Star Is Born, A.** Fredric March, Janet Gaynor, Adolphe Menjou, Andy Devine, Franklin Pangborn. 1937, color, 111 minutes. Remade in 1954 with Judy Garland, James Mason, Charles Bickford (color, 154 minutes). A fading male screen star (March/Mason) marries a talented young protegee (Gaynor/Garland) and suffers emotional devastation as the woman's career blossoms. The 1930s classic was remade in 1954 as a dynamic musical showcase for Garland and again in 1976 with a rock music setting (starring Barbra Streisand and Kris Kristofferson). The first two are excellent backstage dramas; the 1974 effort is a real turkey. Both versions listed here are not rated, and are most appreciated by ages fourteen and over. (See page 80.)

■ **Start the Revolution without Me.** Gene Wilder, Donald Sutherland, Hugh Griffith, Billie Whitelaw, Victor Spinetti, Ewa Aulin. 1970, color, 91 minutes. Two sets of twins (one of nobility, the other of peasant stock) switched at birth are reunited in the intrigue-filled court of Louis XVI at the time of the French Revolution. A little-known comic gem well-performed by Sutherland and Wilder as both sets of twins. Rated PG. Recommended for all ages. (See page 40.)

■ **State of the Union.** Spencer Tracy, Katharine Hepburn, Angela Lansbury, Van Johnson. 1948, B&W, 124 minutes. Prominent businessman Tracy is drafted to run for president and forced to confront issues of character and integrity by his tough-minded spouse Hepburn. One of the most substantial of the great Tracy-Hepburn collaborations, this film version of a popular Broadway play also gives insight into the presidential nomination process when it was controlled by party bosses. Lansbury, star of television's "Murder, She Wrote," plays a wealthy campaign contributor. Not rated. Recommended for all ages. (See page 109.)

■ **Sullivan's Travels.** Joel McCrea, Veronica Lake, William Demarest, Franklin Pangborn. 1941, B&W, 91 minutes. Tough, ambitious movie director McCrae wants to switch from comedy and make an "epic about misery," first going out into the world in hobo rags and with only a dime in his pocket. Rowdy satire about the gap between movie fantasy and workaday reality, from hugely talented writer/director Preston Sturges. Not rated. Most appreciated by ages twelve and over. (See page 79.)

■ **Sunset Boulevard.** William Holden, Gloria Swanson, Erich Von Stroheim, Jack Webb, Nancy Olson, Cecil B. DeMille. 1950, B&W, 110 minutes. Out-of-work screenwriter Holden is taken in by faded star Swanson as they work on the script for her never-to-be comeback picture. This satirical behind-the-scenes look at mid-century Hollywood is renowned for its elegant wit, juicy performances, and opulent decadence. The scene of Swanson revisiting her long-ago studio and being lovingly (if patronizingly) welcomed by DeMille is a charmer. Not rated. Most appreciated by ages twelve and over. (See page 80.)

■ **Sweet Dreams.** Jessica Lange, Ed Harris. 1985, color, 115 minutes. Patsy Cline elevated female country music performers' stature in the 1950s, writing and singing of real-life heartache in piercing, plaintive tones. This hard-hitting film bio defines the Cline mystique and depicts the sources of some of her woes. Lange excels at capturing Cline's physical and emotional lushness and lip-syncs to original Cline recordings. Rated PG. Most appreciated by ages twelve and over. (See page 95.)

■ **Sweet Smell of Success, The.** Burt Lancaster, Tony Curtis, Martin Milner, Susan Harrison. 1957, B&W, 96 minutes. Malicious New York nightlife columnist Lancaster uses his journalistic power to build up and destroy performers and to manipulate the lives of those around him. Gritty, acerbic look at a time when gossip columnists held sway over New York and Hollywood. Milner was later the costar of television's "Route 66," and "Adam 12." Not rated. Most appreciated by ages twelve and over. (See page 105.)

■ **Tell Them Willie Boy Is Here.** Robert Redford, Robert Blake, Katharine Ross, Susan Clark. 1969, color, 96 minutes. Paiute Indian firebrand Blake slays a tribal elder in a dispute over his love for Ross. When the couple escapes into the southwest wilderness, overzealous white lawmen turn the incident into a national emergency. Based on an event that occurred in 1912, the movie dramatizes abuse and prejudice toward Native Americans in the context of traditional chase-action drama. Redford plays a soft-hearted U.S. marshal. Rated PG. Recommended for all ages. (See page 73.)

■ **Tim.** Mel Gibson, Piper Laurie. 1979, color, 108 minutes. Simple, affecting story of a mentally-challenged Australian laborer (Gibson) who becomes the friend, then the husband, of a sensitive spinster (Laurie). This soap opera romance has a rich, nicely depicted touch of family drama, in Tim's interaction with his parents and sister. Rated PG. Most appreciated by ages twelve and over. (See page 61.)

■ **To Hell and Back.** Audie Murphy, Susan Kohner, Jack Kelly, David Janssen. 1955, B&W, 106 minutes. Battle-by-battle story of Audie Murphy, the Texas farm boy who became the most decorated U.S. soldier in World War II. Murphy's playing himself lends a note of authenticity to a fine foxhole-level view of war. Murphy went on to perform ably in more than forty films, primarily Westerns. Not rated. Recommended for all ages. (See page 58.)

■ **To Kill a Mockingbird.** Gregory Peck, Brock Peters, Mary Badham, Philip Alford, Robert Duvall. 1962, B&W, 129 minutes. Two young children (Badham and Alford) look on as their lawyer father (Peck) defends a black man accused of assaulting a white woman in a small southern town in the 1930s. Important social issues involving prejudice, fear, and distrust are presented with evenhanded intelligence, as the story is convincingly told from the children's point of view. Robert Duvall has a memorable bit part as a mysterious neighbor whom everyone fears and the children befriend. A must-see family film. Oscar: Best actor (Peck). Not rated. Recommended for all ages. (See page 53.)

■ **Tootsie.** Dustin Hoffman, Jessica Lange, Teri Garr, Dabney Coleman, Bill Murray, Charles Durning. 1982, color, 116 minutes. Struggling actor Hoffman poses as a middle-aged woman to win a lucrative soap opera role, and in the process creates a personality, named Dorothy Michaels, affecting the lives of those around him/her. A most challenging comedy executed with daring brilliance. Hoffman is amazing. Oscar: Best supporting actress (Lange). Rated PG. Most appreciated by ages eight and over. (See page 40.)

■ **Topper.** Cary Grant, Constance Bennett, Roland Young, Billie Burke, Alan Mowbray. 1937, B&W/colorized, 97 minutes. Following their deaths in a car accident, Grant and Bennett decide to occupy their hereafter hours by juicing up the dull life of their stuffy banker friend, Cosmo Topper (Young). Splendid, irresistible fun, and the ideal film to introduce youngsters to 1930s and '40s comedies. Not rated. Recommended for all ages. (See page 37.)

■ **Tree Grows in Brooklyn, A.** Peggy Ann Garner, Dorothy McGuire, Joan Blondell, James Dunn, Lloyd Nolan. 1945, B&W, 128 minutes. Hardscrabble life in New York City's turn-of-the-century slums is presented through the eyes of the precocious daughter of a down-trodden tenement family. This unadorned adaptation of Betty Smith's famous coming-of-age novel captures the wide-eyed optimism of young Jennie (Garner) as she upholds her values amid squalor and adversity. Oscars: Best supporting actor (Dunn), special recognition award (Garner). Not rated. Recommended for all ages. (See page 100.)

■ **Tremors.** Kevin Bacon, Fred Ward, Michael Gross, Reba McEntire. 1990, color, 96 minutes. Citizens of a small Southwest town are terrorized by four huge burrowing reptiles and must figure out how to thwart the beasts – *fast.* Pulpy sci-fi horror flick handled with great style and high humor. Rated PG-13 for frequent mild profanity. A great hoot for everyone in the family not spooked by lizard-tongued mole monsters. (See page 48.)

■ **True Grit.** John Wayne, Kim Darby, Glen Campbell, Robert Duvall, Strother Martin. 1969, color, 128 minutes. Spunky young Arkansas girl Maddie Ross (Darby) hires notorious drunkard bounty hunter Rooster Cogburn (Wayne) to help track down the man who murdered her father. This warm, affectionate, humorous, and action-filled Western focuses on the evolving relationship between Maddie and Rooster. Followed by a sequel, *Rooster Cogburn,* which is not as successful a piece of filmmaking, although it does pair Wayne with Katharine Hepburn. Oscar: Best actor (Wayne). Rated G. Recommended for all ages. (See page 75.)

■ **Twelve Angry Men.** Henry Fonda, Lee J. Cobb, Ed Begley, E. G. Marshall, Jack Klugman, Jack Warden, Martin Balsam. 1957, B&W, 95 minutes. The lone holdout on a murder-trial jury convinces the other eleven jury members to listen to his arguments. Superbly realistic drama of the American jury system at work, with all-around excellent performances by several yet-to-be-famous actors. Not rated. Most appreciated by ages ten and over. (See page 91.)

■ **2001: A Space Odyssey.** Keir Dullea, Gary Lockwood, William Sylvester. 1968, color, 139 minutes. A space mission following the trail of extraterrestrial contact to the moons of Jupiter is taken over by a renegade computer, ultimately causing lone survivor Dullea to go hurtling into a netherworld of mystery and fascination. Setting out to make the definitive sci-fi space adventure, director Stanley Kubrick selected as his theme nothing less than man's being and becoming (it opens with the dawn of man). His special effects hold up spectacularly well after twenty-plus years. One of the all-time great movies. Rated G. Recommended for all ages. (See page 88.)

■ **2010.** Roy Scheider, Keir Dullea, John Lithgow, Helen Mirren, Bob Balaban. 1984, color, 114 minutes. This sequel plots a follow-up space journey to uncover the fate of the craft and crew in *2001,* in the process explaining all the delightful mysteries and enigmas of the previous film. Still a watchable sci-fi adventure that manages to retain a proper sense of awe in the face of its dogged literalness. Rated PG. Recommended for all ages. (See page 88.)

■ **Under Fire.** Nick Nolte, Gene Hackman, Joanna Cassidy, Ed Harris. 1983, color, 128 minutes. Three globe-trotting journalists come to Nicaragua in the late 1970s to cover the Sandanistas' triumphant campaign against the Somoza government. This zesty, trenchant action-adventure movie shows how journalists can use and be used by their subjects. Great atmospherics and ensemble acting. Rated R for profanity and violence. Most appreciated by ages fourteen and over. (See page 107.)

■ **Viva Zapata!** Marlon Brando, Jean Peters, Anthony Quinn. 1952, B&W, 113 minutes. The rise of Emiliano Zapata from dispossessed peasant farmer to guerrilla leader in early twentieth century Mexico is recounted in a moving film tribute notable for its sweaty realism and starry-eyed look at the revolutionary character. Brando's performance as Zapata is one of his half dozen must-see roles. Oscar: Best supporting actor (Quinn). Not rated. Recommended for all ages. (See page 56.)

■ **Wait Until Dark.** Audrey Hepburn, Alan Arkin, Richard Crenna, Efrem Zimbalist, Jr., Jack Weston. 1967, color, 108 minutes. Blind Manhattan housewife Hepburn tries to outwit the trio of bad guys looking for a heroin cache that has mistakenly fallen into her husband's (Zimbalist) hands. Clever use of the attributes of sightlessness in crafting a taut, chilling thriller. Not rated. Recommended for all ages. (See page 63.)

■ **WarGames.** Matthew Broderick, Dabney Coleman, Ally Sheedy, John Wood. 1983, color, 110 minutes. Boy genius Broderick inadvertently taps into U.S. government computer network, innocently begins to play "Global Thermonuclear Warfare" exercise, and brings the nation to the brink of annihilation. Smart, sometimes irresponsible anticomputer film, with clever performances by the principals. Rated PG. Recommended for all ages. (See page 88.)

■ **War of the Worlds.** Gene Barry, Anne Robinson. 1953, color, 85 minutes. Formidable alien crafts land outside Los Angeles, establish a command post, and begin directing a global assault on civilization. Armies cannot defeat them. Bombs and other modern weapons are useless. What can the earthlings do? This quintessential sci-fi adventure is executed with brainy style and still-convincing special effects. Not rated. Recommended for all ages. (See page 49.)

■ **West Side Story.** Natalie Wood, Richard Beymer, Rita Moreno, George Chakiris, Russ Tamblyn. 1961, color, 151 minutes. Tony (Beymer) and Maria (Wood) find true love on New York's Upper West Side amid bloody conflict involving their combative ethnic tribes, the cops, and society at large. This improbable, enduring romance between the children of warring factions and families, a familiar dramatic staple, has never been more stirringly expressed than in this soaring, revolutionary musical sensation. Music by Leonard Bernstein, lyrics by Stephen Sondheim, choreography by Jerome Robbins. Oscar: Best director, Jerome Robbins and Robert Wise. Not rated. Recommended for all ages. (See page 45.)

■ **Wild One, The.** Marlon Brando, Lee Marvin, Mary Murphy, Jay C. Flippen. 1954, B&W, 79 minutes. A marauding biker gang takes over a sleepy California town and makes life a living hell for the local rubes. The film that brought the post-war Hells Angels-style outlaw phenomenon to broad public attention in colorful, albeit soft-pedaled (no drugs) terms. Flavorful performances by Brando and Marvin as leaders of rival gangs. Not rated. Most appreciated by ages eight and over. (See page 44.)

■ **Will Penny.** Charlton Heston, Joan Hackett, Donald Pleasance, Lee Majors, Bruce Dern, Slim Pickens, Ben Johnson. 1968, color, 108 minutes. Aging cowpoke Heston hooks up with a woman and her son on their way west and must face down a band of unusually nasty toughs. Impressively unglamorized look at cowboys and cowboy life features Heston in his most underplayed and appealing role. Not rated. Recommended for all ages. (See page 75.)

■ **Witness for the Prosecution.** Marlene Dietrich, Tyrone Power, Charles Laughton, Elsa Lanchester. 1957, B&W, 114 minutes. Engaging, intricate British courtroom intrigue involving the case of an ambitious inventor/entrepreneur accused of murdering a wealthy benefactress. Based on an Agatha Christie play and filled with the author's characteristic twists and turns. Rich with detail of centuries-old British legal custom and practice. Not rated. Most appreciated by ages twelve and over. (See page 91.)

■ **Wolf Man, The.** Lon Chaney, Jr., Claude Rains, Ralph Bellamy, Maria Ouspenskaya, Bela Lugosi. 1941, B&W, 70 minutes. Nice guy Chaney is bitten by werewolf Lugosi one night in an English forest and must endure the curse of lycanthropy himself. Believable story, likable characters, and crackerjack special effects make this one of the most well-rounded monster classics. Not rated. Recommended for all ages. (See page 47.)

■ **Yankee Doodle Dandy.** James Cagney, Walter Huston, Joan Leslie, Irene Manning, Rosemary DeCamp. 1942, B&W, 126 minutes. Wonderfully affectionate musical biography of composer/performer George M. Cohan, source of standards such as "Over There," "Give My Regards to Broadway," and "It's a Grand Old Flag." Offers outstanding insight into early twentieth-century popular music, as Cohan rises from vaudeville performances with his parents and sister to multihit Broadway stardom. Knockout performance by James Cagney, best known for his gangster roles, shows his roots as a vaudeville dancer. The title song production number is one of the finest Hollywood musical moments ever. Oscar: Best actor (Cagney). Not rated. Recommended for all ages. (See page 92.)

■ **Year of Living Dangerously, The.** Mel Gibson, Sigourney Weaver, Linda Hunt, Michael Murphy. 1983, color, 115 minutes. Australian radio journalist Gibson is assigned to Jakarta in the last days of Indonesia's Sukarno dictatorship and uncovers a rebel plot to smuggle arms into the country. Rare and effective depiction of social, economic, and political conditions in a Third World nation and the issues the West confronts in dealing with them. Notable for two performances: Gibson, before he became a mega action-adventure star, and American stage actress Hunt as the dwarfish male photographer Billy Kwan. Oscar: Best supporting actress (Hunt). Rated R for infrequent profanity and sexual content, including nudity. Most appreciated by ages fourteen and over. (See page 107.)

■ **Yellow Submarine.** 1968, color, 85 minutes. In the 1960s, it sometimes seemed as if everything the Beatles touched was a magical delight, and this animated feature, directed by George Dunning, they barely touched at all. Frolicsome Beatles songs are used throughout the fanciful fairy tale that has characters based on John, Paul, George, and Ringo battling ogres, known as the Blue

Meanies, who want to conquer idyllic Pepperland. Jam-packed with visual and verbal puns, the movie can be enjoyed repeatedly for its intricate, original wit. A wonderful experience for young children. Not rated. Recommended for all ages. (See page 97.)

■ **Young Frankenstein.** Gene Wilder, Peter Boyle, Marty Feldman, Teri Garr, Madeline Kahn, Cloris Leachman, Kenneth Marrs. 1974, B&W, 105 minutes. Frankenstein heir Wilder, trying to live down the family's notoriety, revisits his ancestor's middle-European castle and is smitten by the monster-building urge all over again. Writer-director Mel Brooks's funniest movie parody is like a dingy old attic full of wacky treasures and zany creations. After three or four viewings you're still finding new things to laugh at. Rated PG. Recommended for all ages. (See page 47.)

■ **Young Man with a Horn.** Kirk Douglas, Lauren Bacall, Doris Day, Hoagy Carmichael. 1950, B&W, 112 minutes. Innovative jazz trumpeter Douglas, in a character based on musical legend Bix Beiderbecke, challenges mainstream music conventions to establish his own hot-licks sound. Day is the good-girl band singer and Bacall the sultry vixen who distracts Douglas from his musical mission. Valuable perspective on a watershed period in American popular music. Not rated. Most appreciated by ages twelve and over. (See page 94.)

Global Hot Spots:
Selected Movies for
Older Children

As the 1991 film *J.F.K.* showed so dramatically, motion pictures that deal with controversial real-world events are uniquely capable of sparking intense discussion over the events themselves. While most of the viewing public understands that such movies are and always will be "make believe" – freely manipulating history in the interest of providing commercial entertainment – these films can nonetheless be a valuable means of opening discussion with older children about past and present world events.

Following is a list of several world historical events of the past forty-plus years that continue to impact current headline situations. These films are presented with the caveat that, as they deal with contemporary affairs, many of them contain profanity, sexual content, and scenes of violence that make them unsuitable for blanket endorsement as family viewing. They are presented here as a guideline to parents who nevertheless are interested in viewing movies about global hot spots with their teenaged children, objectionable content notwithstanding.

South Africa

■ **Cry Freedom.** Denzel Washington, Kevin Kline, Zakes Mokae, Alec McCowen. 1987, color, 157 minutes. Heroic story of black South African activist Steven Biko (Washington), his death in prison, and the efforts of white journalist Donald Woods (Kline) to tell Biko's story. This lengthy, faithfully detailed account of true events was criticized for its overemphasis on Woods, who was forced to abandon his family and flee South Africa because of his activities. Still, a rare, sensitive look at the racial tinderbox of South Africa. Rated PG for infrequent, moderate violence. Most appreciated by ages twelve and over. (Also see page 107.)

■ **Dry, White Season, A.** Donald Sutherland, Janet Suzman, Zakes Mokae, Jurgen Prochnow, Susan Sarandon, Marlon Brando. 1989, color, 107 minutes. A conservative white South African schoolteacher (Sutherland) is awakened to the terror blacks face in his country when a black colleague's son is killed by police, and Sutherland cannot find out who is responsible. Rare major film tackling one of the world's most heinous social problems, primarily told from perspective of its impact on young people. Brando is unforgettable as an obstreperous liberal lawyer. Rated R for infrequent profanity and violence. Most appreciated by ages twelve and over.

Middle East

■ **Exodus.** Paul Newman, Eva Marie Saint, Sal Mineo, Peter Lawford, Lee J. Cobb, Hugh Griffith, John Derek, Jill Haworth. 1960, color, 213 minutes. Monumental epic, almost four hours long, tracing the post-World War II events surrounding the establishment of an independent Jewish state on Palestinian territory. Lengthy, worthwhile (if unthinkingly pro-Israel) primer on the root causes of continuing Israeli-Palestinian tensions. Not rated. Most appreciated by ages twelve and over.

■ **Little Drummer Girl.** Diane Keaton, Klaus Kinski, Sami Frey. 1984, color, 130 minutes. A professional stage actress (Keaton) is recruited by Israeli intelligence to infiltrate Palestinian terrorist ranks and betray the guerrilla leader. Based on a novel by former British intelligence operative John Le Carre, the story is believed to depict faithfully, if not literally, Israel's extraordinary efforts to track down the Arabs responsible for the massacre of eleven Israeli athletes at the 1972 Summer Olympics. True or not, this story takes you on a heart-pounding ride through the dark alleys of Arab-Israeli relations. Rated R for profanity, violence, and sexual content, including nudity. Most appreciated by ages fourteen and over.

Modern Communism

■ **Doctor Zhivago.** Julie Christie, Omar Sharif, Rod Steiger, Alec Guinness, Tom Courtenay, Rita Tushingham. 1965, color, 180 minutes. Memorable romance of Christie and Sharif is set against historic events before, during, and after the Russian Revolution that established Communist rule in the USSR. Shaky history perhaps, but magnificent spectacle. Christie is mesmerizing. Not rated. Most appreciated by ages ten and over.

■ **October** (also, **Ten Days That Shook The World**). 1928, B&W, 103 minutes. Esteemed Soviet director Sergei Eisenstein's dramatic, documentary-style recreation of the climactic events of the 1917 Bolshevik Revolution that brought the Russian Communists to power. Inspired by the book-length report by American leftist journalist John Reed, subject of the Warren Beatty feature film *Reds* (see below). Not rated. Most appreciated by ages eight and over.

■ **Potemkin** (also, **Battleship Potemkin**). 1925, B&W, 65 minutes. A Russian battleship crew's rebellion against tyrannical officers in 1905, presented as a microcosm and precursor of the Bolshevik Revolution in 1917. Also directed by Sergei Eisenstein, and justifiably one of the most highly regarded films ever made. It captures the people's revulsion at czarist oppression with you-are-there film-making and a story that still excites more than sixty-five years later. Made as a postrevolution pro-Soviet propaganda piece. Not rated. Can be appreciated by all ages, but mostly by ages twelve and over.

■ **Reds.** Warren Beatty, Diane Keaton, Jack Nicholson, Maureen Stapleton, Edward Herrmann, Gene Hackman, William Daniels. 1981, color, 201 minutes. The early activist/intellectual roots of American communism are captured in the story of journalist John Reed (see *October*) and his relationship with dilettante artist/author Louise Bryant, playwright Eugene O'Neill, labor leader Emma Goldman, and others. Sweeping historical drama interspersed with brief talking-head interviews with some real-life participants. Oscars: Best director (Beatty), supporting actress (Stapleton). Rated PG for infrequent profanity, wartime violence, and sexual dialogue. Most appreciated by ages fourteen and over.

Vietnam and Southeast Asia

■ **Apocalypse Now.** Marlon Brando, Martin Sheen, Robert Duvall, Frederic Forest, Dennis Hopper, Larry Fishburne. 1979, color, 150 minutes. U.S. intelligence operative Sheen travels upriver through war-torn Vietnam and into Cambodia on an assignment to assassinate renegade Army officer Brando. He experiences a series of slam-bang vignettes along the way that defines the madness of the American Vietnam experience. Director Francis Coppola's magnificent spectacle is the best Vietnam movie to date, largely because he frames the U.S. debacle in terms of cultural ignorance rather than faulty military or geopolitical strategy. A film whose reputation is growing as time passes. Rated R for frequent harsh profanity and extreme violence. Most appreciated by ages fourteen and over (and even then an understanding of the subject matter is essential).

■ **Coming Home.** Jane Fonda, Jon Voight, Bruce Dern. 1978, color, 127 minutes. Stateside hospital volunteer Fonda falls in love with patient Voight, a paraplegic Vietnam veteran, and then must explain matters to her gung-ho officer husband Dern on his return from the war. This popular antiwar drama was the first movie to deal extensively with the challenges of returning Vietnam veterans. Oscars: Best actress (Fonda), actor (Voight). Rated R for profanity and sexual content, including nudity. Most appreciated by ages fourteen and over.

■ **Go Tell the Spartans.** Burt Lancaster, Craig Wasson, Marc Singer. 1978, color, 114 minutes. U.S. Army major (Lancaster) begins to doubt America's Vietnam strategy early in the war (1964) and grows more cynical as his men are ordered to secure an abandoned Vietnamese village. Standard battlefield action is mixed with pointed political commentary and broadly satirical humor. An appealing sleeper. Rated R for infrequent harsh profanity and battlefield violence. Most appreciated by ages twelve and over.

■ **Green Berets, The.** John Wayne, David Janssen, Jim Hutton, Aldo Ray, Raymond St. Jacques. 1968, color, 141 minutes. Conventional, exciting, wartime action-adventure featuring men of the U.S. Special Forces, the first American troops in Vietnam. Notable for being an early and still lonely example of pro-Vietnam movie sentiment. Wayne also directed. Rated G. Can be appreciated by all ages (it deals in part with the war's impact on Vietnamese children), but mostly by ages ten and over.

■ **Killing Fields, The.** Sam Waterston, Haing S. Ngor, John Malkovich, Craig T. Nelson, Julian Sands. 1984, color, 141 minutes. Deeply moving account of Cambodia's fall to Khmer Rouge guerrillas in 1975 and the subsequent efforts of *New York Times* reporter Sidney Schanberg (Waterston) to help locate native Cambodian news photographer Dith Pran (Ngor) after the rebel takeover. Impressive account of the fugitive's battle for survival and a valuable perspective usually omitted from pictures dealing with revolutions: what happens after the rebels come to power? Rated R for infrequent violence and some disturbing scenes. Most appreciated by ages fourteen and over.

■ **Ugly American, The.** Marlon Brando, Sandra Church, Pat Hingle, Arthur Hill, Eiji Okada. 1963, color, 120 minutes. Film based on the controversial 1962 Burdick-Lederer novel, which chronicles American diplomatic bungling in Southeast Asia following the French pullout in the mid-1950s. Perceptively anticipates many of the issues that surfaced later in the Vietnam War and attempts to identify the social underpinnings of the mass support for the Viet Cong guerrillas. Brando plays the fictional U.S. ambassador around whom the conflict swirls. Not rated. Most appreciated by ages fourteen and over.

■ **Day of the Jackal, The.** Edward Fox, Alan Badel, Cyril Cusack. 1973, color, 141 minutes. Right-wing French militarists hire crack European mercenary to assassinate President Charles de Gaulle, in retaliation for DeGaulle's having awarded independence to the former French African colony of Algeria. This taut thriller is based on a novel by Frederick Forsytge, and is said to be closely based on actual (and unsuccessful) attempts on DeGaulle's life in the early 1960s. The movie is a virtual minute-by-minute account of the assassin's preparations and maneuvers, and French police efforts to identify and stop him. Blistering action drama. Rated PG for infrequent violence and modest sexual content. Most appreciated by ages twelve and up.

■ **Z.** Yves Montand, Irene Papas, Jean-Louis Trintignant. 1969, color, 127. Classic political melodrama, inspired by real events in Greece in the 1960s, as the military overthrew a civilian government and installed an onerous dictatorship. Popular political figure (Montand) is assassinated by his opponents, and an incorruptible young government lawyer (Trintignant) tries to get to the bottom of the murder, without regard to bureaucratic ciceties. Rated PG. Most appreciated by ages twelve and up.

Performers' Directory

Just about everyone has a favorite movie actor or actress, and so, too, very likely will you and your children come to look forward to the work of certain actors. Many video stores now display movies grouped by performer. To assist you in selecting movies by your family's favorite actors, we have compiled a list of popular performers and their movies – both those we discuss in this book (which have an asterisk), as well as others that merit consideration for family viewing. The movies listed below have ratings of G, PG, PG-13, or R, so readers are strongly encouraged to consult comprehensive movie guides, such as those listed in Appendix C, for complete content and rating information on titles not discussed elsewhere in this book.

Allen, Woody (1935-   )

*Bananas**
*Broadway Danny Rose**
Casino Royale
Purple Rose of Cairo, The
Sleeper

Take the Money and Run
What's New, Pussycat?
What's Up, Tigerlily?
Zelig

Bergman, Ingrid (1915-1982)

Anastasia
Bells of St. Mary's, The
Cactus Flower
*Casablanca**
Gaslight
Inn of the Sixth Happiness, The

Intermezzo
Joan of Arc
Notorious
Murder on the Orient Express
Spellbound

Bogart, Humphrey (1899-1957)

Across the Pacific
African Queen, The
*Angels With Dirty Faces**
Barefoot Contessa, The
Beat the Devil
Big Sleep, The

*Caine Mutiny, The**
*Casablanca**
Harder They Fall, The
High Sierra
Key Largo
Maltese Falcon, The

Oklahoma Kid, The
Petrified Forest, The
Roaring Twenties, The

Sahara
To Have and Have Not
Treasure of the Sierra Madre, The

Brando, Marlon (1924-   )

Chase, The
Julius Caesar
Mutiny on the Bounty, The
One-Eyed Jacks
*On the Waterfront**
*Superman**

Teahouse of the August Moon, The
*Ugly American, The**
*Viva Zapata!**
*Wild One, The**
Young Lions, The

Cagney, James (1899-1986)

*Angels With Dirty Faces**
Footlight Parade
*Love Me or Leave Me**
Oklahoma Kid, The
*Midsummer Night's Dream, A**
*Mister Roberts**

One Two Three
Public Enemy
Roaring Twenties, The
Strawberry Blonde
White Heat
*Yankee Doodle Dandy**

Chaplin, Charles (1889-1977)

Circus, The
City Lights
*Gold Rush, The**
Great Dictator, The

Limelight
*Modern Times**
Monsieur Verdoux

(Several anthologies of short Chaplin features are also available on video.)

Connery, Sean (1929-   )

Bridge Too Far, A
Diamonds Are Forever
Doctor No
From Russia with Love
Goldfinger
Hill, The
*Longest Day, The**

*Man Who Would Be King, The**
Murder on the Orient Express
Never Say Never Again
*Robin and Marian**
Russia House
Thunderball
You Only Live Twice

Cooper, Gary (1901-1961)

Beau Geste
Farewell to Arms
Friendly Persuasion
*High Noon**
Lives of a Bengal Lancer

Meet John Doe
Mr. Deeds Goes to Town
Plainsman, The
Pride of the Yankees
*Sergeant York**

Vera Cruz
Westerner, The

Wreck of the Mary Deare, The

Costner, Kevin

American Flyers
*Dances With Wolves**
*Field of Dreams**

Robin Hood: Prince of Thieves
Silverado

Curtis, Tony (1925-   )

*Defiant Ones, The**
Great Race, The
Houdini
*Operation Petticoat**
*Some Like It Hot**

*Spartacus**
*Sweet Smell of Success, The**
Trapeze
Vikings, The

Douglas, Kirk (1916-   )

Ace in the Hole
*Bad and the Beautiful, The**
Champion
Detective Story
*Gunfight at the OK Corral**
Lust for Life
*Lonely Are the Brave**
Man from Snowy River, The

Paths of Glory
*Seven Days in May**
*Spartacus**
*20,000 Leagues Under the Sea**
Ulysses
Vikings, The
War Wagon, The
*Young Man with a Horn**

Field, Sally (1946-   )

*Absence of Malice**
*Norma Rae**
*Places in the Heart**

Smokey and the Bandit
Steel Magnolias
Stay Hungry

Flynn, Errol (1909-1959)

*Adventures of Robin Hood, The**
Captain Blood
Charge of the Light Brigade, The
Dawn Patrol, The

Gentleman Jim
*Sea Hawk**
They Died with Their Boots On

Fonda, Henry (1905-1982)

*Advise and Consent**
*Best Man, The**
Big Hand for a Little Lady
Drums Along the Mohawk
*Fail-Safe**
Grapes of Wrath, The

How the West Was Won
*Longest Day, The**
*Mister Roberts**
*My Darling Clementine**
Once Upon a Time in the West
*On Golden Pond**

Ox Bow Incident, The
Return of Frank James, The

*Twelve Angry Men**
Young Mr. Lincoln

Fonda, Jane (1937-   )

*Cat Ballou**
Chase, The
*China Syndrome, The**

*Coming Home**
*On Golden Pond**
They Shoot Horses Don't They

Ford, Harrison (1942-   )

*American Graffiti**
Blade Runner
*Empire Strikes Back, The**
Indiana Jones and the Last Crusade
Indiana Jones and the Temple of
    Doom

*Mosquito Coast, The**
*Raiders of the Lost Ark**
*Return of the Jedi**
*Star Wars**
Witness

Freeman, Morgan

Driving Miss Daisy
*Glory**

Lean on Me
Robin Hood: Prince of Thieves

Gibson, Mel (1956-   )

Bounty, The
Gallipoli
Hamlet

River, The
*Tim**
*Year of Living Dangerously, The**

Grant, Cary (1904-1986)

Arsenic and Old Lace
*Awful Truth, The**
Bringing Up Baby
Charade
Destination Tokyo
Gunga Din
*His Girl Friday**
Holiday
Mr. Blandings Builds His Dream
    House

North by Northwest
Notorious
*Operation Petticoat**
*Philadelphia Story, The**
Suspicion
To Catch a Thief
*Topper**

Guinness, Alec (1914-   )

*Bridge on the River Kwai, The**
*Doctor Zhivago**
*Empire Strikes Back, The**
Father Brown
Lavender Hill Mob, The

*Lawrence of Arabia**
Man in the White Suit, The
Quiller Memorandum, The
*Star Wars**
Tunes of Glory

Hepburn, Audrey (1929-   )

Charade	*Robin and Marian**
Funny Face	*Roman Holiday*
*My Fair Lady**	*Wait Until Dark**
Nun's Story, The	*War and Peace*

Hepburn, Katharine (1907-   )

*Adam's Rib**	*On Golden Pond**
African Queen, The	*Pat and Mike*
Bringing Up Baby	*Philadelphia Story, The**
Desk Set	*Rooster Cogburn*
*Guess Who's Coming to Dinner**	*Stage Door**
Holiday	*State of the Union, The**
Lion in Winter, The	*Woman of the Year*
Little Women	

Holden, William (1918-1981)

*Bridge on the River Kwai, The**	*Network*
Bridges at Toko-Ri, The	*Stalag 17*
Golden Boy	*Sunset Boulevard**
Horse Soldiers, The	*Wild Rovers, The*
Our Town	

Karloff, Boris (1887-1969)

Black Room, The	*Mummy, The*
Body Snatcher, The	*Raven, The*
*Bride of Frankenstein, The**	*Son of Frankenstein*
Charlie Chan at the Opera	*Targets*
*Frankenstein**	

Kelly, Gene (1912-   )

An American in Paris	*Pirate, The*
Anchors Away	*Singin' in the Rain**
Cover Girl	*That's Entertainment**
*Inherit the Wind**	*Three Musketeers, The*
On the Town	*Take Me Out to the Ball Game*

Lancaster, Burt (1913-   )

Airport	*Go Tell the Spartans**
Bird Man of Alcatraz, The	*Gunfight at the OK Corral**
Elmer Gantry	*Judgement at Nuremburg**
Flame and the Arrow, The	*Killers, The*

Local Hero
Professionals, The
Run Silent, Run Deep
Seven Days in May*

Sweet Smell of Success, The*
Trapeze
Vera Cruz

Lemmon, Jack (1925-   )

China Syndrome, The*
Dad
Fortune Cookie, The
Great Race, The

Mister Roberts*
Odd Couple, The*
Some Like It Hot*
Wackiest Ship in the Army, The

Marx Brothers

Animal Crackers
At the Circus
Big Store, The
Coconuts, The
Day at the Races, A
Duck Soup*

Go West
Horse Feathers
Monkey Business
Night at the Opera, A*
Night in Casablanca, A
Room Service

Matthau, Walter (1920-   )

Bad News Bears, The
Charade
Face in the Crowd, A*
Fail-Safe*
First Monday in October, The*
Fortune Cookie, The
Hello Dolly
Hopscotch

Kotch
Lonely Are the Brave*
Odd Couple, The*
Plaza Suite
Sunshine Boys, The
Taking of Pelham One Two Three,
    The

Newman, Paul (1925-   )

Absence of Malice*
Butch Cassidy and the Sundance
    Kid*
Cool Hand Luke
Exodus*
Harper
Hombre

Hud*
Hustler, The
Judge Roy Bean
Left-Handed Gun, The
Somebody Up There Likes Me
Sting, The
Verdict, The

O'Toole, Peter (1932-   )

Becket
Casino Royale
Goodbye Mr. Chips

Lawrence of Arabia*
Lion in Winter, The
Lord Jim

My Favorite Year
Stunt Man, The

What's New, Pussycat?

Peck, Gregory (1916-   )

Big Country, The
Duel in the Sun
Guns of Navarone, The
Gunfighter, The
How the West Was Won
Keys to the Kingdom, The
*MacArthur**
*Moby Dick**

On the Beach
Pork Chop Hill
Roman Holiday
Spellbound
*To Kill a Mockingbird**
Twelve O'Clock High
*Yearling, The**

Poitier, Sidney (1924-   )

Bedford Incident, The
*Blackboard Jungle, The**
*Defiant Ones, The**
*Guess Who's Coming to Dinner**
*In the Heat of the Night**
*Lillies of the Field**
Little Nikita

Patch of Blue, A
Raisin in the Sun, A
*Separate But Equal**
Shoot to Kill
To Sir with Love
Willby Conspiracy, The

Quinn, Anthony (1915-   )

Guns of Navarone, The
Hunchback of Notre Dame, The
*Lawrence of Arabia**
Lust For Life
Requiem For a Heavyweight

Secret of Santa Vittoria, The
Ulysses
*Viva Zapata!**
Zorba the Greek

Redford, Robert (1936-   )

*All the President's Men**
Barefoot in the Park
Bridge Too Far, A
Brubaker
*Butch Cassidy and the Sundance
    Kid**
Chase, The
*Candidate, The**

Downhill Racer
*Jeremiah Johnson**
*Natural, The**
Out of Africa
Sting, The
*Tell Them Willie Boy Is Here**
Three Days of the Condor

Robinson, Edward G. (1893-1973)

*Cheyenne Autumn**
Cincinnati Kid, The
Hole in the Head
House of Strangers, The

Key Largo
Little Caesar
Sea Wolf, The
Soylent Green

Reynolds, Debbie (1932-   )

How the West Was Won	*Tammy and the Bachelor*
*Singin' in the Rain**	*Unsinkable Molly Brown, The*

Sellers, Peter (1925-1980)

Being There	*Return of the Pink Panther**
*Dr. Strangelove**	*Pink Panther Strikes Again, The**
I'm All Right Jack	*What's New, Pussycat?*
Mouse That Roared, The	*World of Henry Orient, The*

Stewart, James (1908-   )

*Anatomy of a Murder**	*Man Who Shot Liberty Valance, The**
Broken Arrow	*Mr. Hobbs Takes a Vacation*
*Cheyenne Autumn**	*Mr. Smith Goes to Washington**
Destry Rides Again	*Philadelphia Story, The**
Far Country, The	*Rear Window*
FBI Story, The	*Shenandoah**
*Glenn Miller Story, The**	*Shootist, The**
*Greatest Show on Earth, The**	*Shop Around the Corner, The*
*Harvey**	*Spirit of St. Louis, The**
How the West Was Won	*Strategic Air Command*
*It's a Wonderful Life**	*You Can't Take it With You*
Man from Laramie, The	*Vertigo*
*Man Who Knew Too Much, The**	*Winchester 73*

Tracy, Spencer (1900-1967)

*Adam's Rib**	*Judgment at Nuremberg**
*Boys Town**	*Last Hurrah, The**
*Captains Courageous**	*Libeled Lady*
Bad Day at Black Rock	*Northwest Passage*
*Boys' Town**	*Old Man and the Sea, The*
Desk Set, The	*Pat and Mike*
*Father of the Bride**	*San Francisco*
*Guess Who's Coming to Dinner**	*Stanley and Livingstone*
*Inherit the Wind**	*State of the Union**
*It's A Mad, Mad, Mad, Mad World**	*Woman of the Year*

Wayne, John (1907-1979)

Alamo, The	*Horse Soldiers, The*
*Cowboys, The**	*How the West Was Won*
El Dorado	*Longest Day, The**
*Green Berets, The**	*Long Voyage Home, The*

Man Who Shot Liberty Valance, The*
Quiet Man, The
Red River*
Rio Bravo*
Rooster Cogburn
Sands of Iwo Jima
Searchers, The

She Wore a Yellow Ribbon
Shootist, The*
Stagecoach
They Were Expendable
Three Godfathers
True Grit*
War Wagon, The

Widmark, Richard (1914-   )

Bedford Incident, The
Cheyenne Autumn*
Coma*
Frogmen, The
How the West Was Won
Judgment at Nuremberg*

Kiss of Death
Madigan
Murder on the Orient Express
Panic in the Streets
Saint Joan*

References

Halliwell, Leslie. *Halliwell's Filmgoer's and Video Viewer's Companion.* 9th ed. New York: Charles Scribner's Sons, 1988. Something quite different from the other reference books listed here, this is organized primarily by performer and includes a list of their films (definitive but not comprehensive) and quotes by and about the major stars. Other entries are for noted directors, writers, and for popular film genres and subject matter. An excellent resource and fun reading.

Halliwell, Leslie. *Halliwell's Film Guide.* 7th ed. New York: Harper & Row, 1989. Probably the most comprehensive guide to movies, with special strength in British and other international titles. Noted for Halliwell's pithy and generally on-the-money comments. All movies rated for quality (although most, in his demanding view, deserve no stars at all). No MPAA rating information.

Karren, Howard, ed. *The Premiere Guide to Movies on Video.* New York: Harper Perennial, 1991. Eclectic collection of miscellaneous columns discussing movies according to broad general themes. Some amusing sidebars and offbeat lists. Includes the list of great 1980s movies as selected by leading film critics. No MPAA rating information.

Kael, Pauline. *5001 Nights at the Movies.* New York: Henry Holt, 1991. Kael, until recently the regular movie critic for *The New Yorker,* is the most influential film critic of the past twenty-five years. This collection contains reviews of films going back to the 1930s excerpted from twelve other collections of her reviews.

Maltin, Leonard, Ed. *Leonard Maltin's TV Movies and Video Guide.* New York: Signet, annually since 1986. Sporadically since 1969. Thorough listing of American-made movies and international movies that have been shown in U.S. theaters or on television or have been transferred to video. Includes made-for-TV movies. Generally reliable commentary and a nice eye for trivia. All movies rated. Contains MPAA rating, but no detailed information.

Martin, Mick, and Porter, Marsha. *Video Movie Guide.* New York: Ballantine Books, annual. Comprehensive directory of films available on video and only resource listed here to include reasons for most PG, PG-13, and R MPAA ratings (profanity, violence, sexual content, etc.). Films organized by category, which can lead to some frustrating searches (e.g., *Nashville* is listed as a drama, not a musical, whereas *La Bamba* and *Honeysuckle Rose* are musicals, not drama). Readers should consult the index first. Also cross-referenced by director, cast, and four-star movies. All movies rated.

Index

K

L

More good books from WILLIAMSON PUBLISHING

To order additional copies of *The Family Video Guide,* please enclose $12.95 per copy plus $2.50 shipping and handling. Follow "To Order" instructions on the last page. Thank you.

PARENTS ARE TEACHERS, TOO: Enriching Your Child's First Six Years
by Claudia Jones

Winner of the Parents' Choice Seal of Approval! Be the best teacher your child ever has. Jones shares hundreds of ways to help any child learn in playful home situations. Lots on developing reading, writing, math skills. Plenty on creative and critical thinking, too. A book you'll love using!

192 pages, 6 × 9, illustrations,
Quality paperback, $9.95

MORE PARENTS ARE TEACHERS, TOO: Encouraging Your 6- to 12-Year-Old
by Claudia Jones

Winner of the Parents' Choice Seal of Approval! Help your children be the best they can be! When parents are involved, kids do better. When kids do better, they feel better, too. Here's a wonderfully creative book of ideas, activities, teaching methods, and more to help you help your children over the rough spots and share in their growing joy in achieving. Plenty on reading, writing, math, problem-solving, creative thinking. Everything for parents who want to help but not push their children.

224 pages, 6 × 9, illustrations,
Quality paperback, $10.95

THE HOMEWORK SOLUTION
by Linda Agler Sonna

Put homework responsibilities where they belong — in the student's lap! Here it is! The simple remedy for the millions of parents who are tired of waging the never-ending nightly battle over kids' homework. Dr. Sonna's "One Step Solution" will relieve parents, kids, and their siblings of the ongoing problem within a single month.

192 pages, 6 × 9,
Quality paperback, $10.95

DOING CHILDREN'S MUSEUMS
A Guide to 265 Hands-On Museums
by Joanne Cleaver

Turn an ordinary day into a spontaneous "vacation" by taking a child to some of the 265 participatory children's museums, discovery rooms, and nature centers covered in this newly expanded and updated, one-of-a-kind book. Filled with museum specifics to help you pick and plan the perfect place for the perfect day, Cleaver has created a most valuable resource for anyone who loves kids!

224 pages, 6 × 9, expanded and updated edition
Quality paperback, $13.95

THE KIDS' NATURE BOOK: 365 Indoor/Outdoor Activities and Experiences
by Susan Milord

Winner of the Parents' Choice Gold Award for learning and doing books, *The Kids' Nature Book* is loved by children, grandparents, and friends alike. Simple projects and activities emphasize fun while quietly reinforcing the wonder of the world we all share. Packed with fascinating facts and fun!

160 pages, 11 × 8½, 425 illustrations
Quality paperback, $12.95

KIDS CREATE! Art & Craft Experiences for 3- to 9-year-olds
by Laurie Carlson

What's the most important experience for children ages 3 to 9? Why, it is to create something by themselves. Carlson provides over 150 creative experiences ranging from making dinosaur sculptures to clay cactus gardens, from butterfly puppets to windsocks. Plenty of help for the parents working with the kids, too! A delightfully innovative book that has sold over 150,000 copies.

160 pages, 11 × 8¹/₂, over 400 illustrations,
Quality paperback, $12.95

KIDS & WEEKENDS! Creative Ways to Make Special Days
by Avery Hart and Paul Mantell

Packed with truly creative ways to play, have fun, learn, grow, and build self-esteem and positive relationships, this book is a must for every parent, grandparent, baby-sitter, and teacher. Hart and Mantell will inspire us all to transform some part of every weekend – even if it is only 30 minutes – into a special experience. Everything from backyard nature to putting on a magic show to creating a bird sanctuary to writing a book about yourself to environmentally sound activities indoors and out. Whatever your interests, no matter how busy you are, kids and their families will savor special weekend moments.

176 pages, 11 × 8¹/₂, over 400 illustrations
Quality paperback, $12.95

KIDS COOK! Fabulous Food for the Whole Family
by Sarah Williamson and Zachary Williamson
Kids Cook! is filled with over 150 recipes for great tasting foods that kids can cook for themselves and for their families and friends, too. Recipes from sections like "Breakfast Bonanzas," "Dynamite Dinners," and "Soda Fountain Treats" include real, healthy foods – not cutesy recipes that are no fun to eat. Plus *Nutri Notes, Safety First,* and plenty of special menus for Father's Day, Grandma's Teatime, picnics, and parties. One terrific book!

176 pages, 11 × 8¹/₂, Over 150 recipes, 400 illustrations
Quality paperback, $12.95

KIDS LEARN AMERICA! Bringing Geography to Life with People, Places, & History
by Patricia Gordon and Reed C. Snow

Designed to help increase "geo-literacy," *Kids Learn America!* is not about memorizing. This creative and exciting new book is about making every region of our country come alive from within, about being connected to the earth and the people across this great expanse called America. ·Activities and games targeted to the 50 states plus D.C. and Puerto Rico · The environment and natural resources ·Geographic comparisons ·Fascinating facts, famous people and places of each region. Let us all join together – kids, parents, friends, teachers, grandparents – and put America, its geography, its history, and its heritage back on the map!

176 pages, 11 × 8 1/2, maps, over 400 illustrations
Quality paperback, $12.95

ADVENTURES IN ART: Art & Craft Experiences for 7- to 14-year-olds
by Susan Milord

Imagine an art book that encourages children to explore, to experience, to touch and to see, to learn and to create . . . imagine a true adventure in art. Here's a book that teaches artisans' skills without stifling creativity. Covers making hand-made papers, puppets, masks, paper seascapes, seed art, tin can lantern, berry ink, still life, silk screen, batiking, carving, and so much more. Perfect for the older child. Let the adventure begin!

160 pages, 11 × 8 1/2, 500 illustrations
Quality paperback, $12.95

To Order:
   At your bookstore or order directly from Williamson Publishing. We accept Visa and MasterCard (please include number and expiration date), or send check to:
   Williamson Publishing Company
   Church Hill Road, P.O. Box 185
   Charlotte, Vermont 05445
   Toll-free phone orders with credit cards:
   1-800-234-8791
Please add $2.50 for postage and handling. Satisfaction is guaranteed or full refund without questions or quibbles.

1/93